Faculty Socialization as Cultural Process:
A Mirror of Institutional Commitment

by William G. Tierney and Robert A. Rhoads

ASHE-ERIC Higher Education Report No. 6, 1993

Prepared by

Clearinghouse on Higher Education
The George Washington University

In cooperation with

Association for the Study
of Higher Education

Published by

School of Education and Human Development
The George Washington University

Jonathan D. Fife, Series Editor

Cite as
Tierney, William G., and Robert A. Rhoads. 1994. *Faculty Socialization as Cultural Process: A Mirror of Institutional Commitment.* ASHE-ERIC Higher Education Report No. 93-6. Washington, D.C.: The George Washington University, School of Education and Human Development.

Library of Congress Catalog Card Number 94-66104
ISSN 0884-0040
ISBN 1-878380-27-3

Managing Editor: Bryan Hollister
Manuscript Editor: Alexandra Rockey
Cover design by Michael David Brown, Rockville, Maryland

The ERIC Clearinghouse on Higher Education invites individuals to submit proposals for writing monographs for the *ASHE-ERIC Higher Education Report* series. Proposals must include:
1. A detailed manuscript proposal of not more than five pages.
2. A chapter-by-chapter outline.
3. A 75-word summary to be used by several review committees for the initial screening and rating of each proposal.
4. A vita and a writing sample.

ERIC Clearinghouse on Higher Education
School of Education and Human Development
The George Washington University
One Dupont Circle, Suite 630
Washington, DC 20036-1183

This publication was prepared partially with funding from the Office of Educational Research and Improvement, U.S. Department of Education, under contract no. ED RR-93-0200. The opinions expressed in this report do not necessarily reflect the positions or policies of OERI or the Department.

EXECUTIVE SUMMARY

What Is the Significance of Faculty Socialization?

Over the last two decades, higher education has come under attack. At the center of much of the criticism lies the United States professorate. Some critics believe that faculty emphasize research at the expense of quality teaching. Others believe that faculty fail to adequately address today's diverse student body. In either case, understanding the many roles faculty play in the formal and informal life of college and university settings is critical if we are to improve our academic organizations.

The multiple roles faculty adopt reflect their learning experiences—their socialization. Hence, understanding faculty socialization is imperative if we are to change our academic settings.

How Is Faculty Socialization Conceptualized?

The values, beliefs, and attitudes held by faculty reflect their socialization experiences and, in essence, mirror faculty culture. In examining faculty socialization through faculty culture, we adopt Geertz's view of culture where culture shapes and is shaped by social interaction (1973). To understand faculty socialization—how faculty learn to be faculty—we first must come to terms with the cultural forces which shape faculty life: the national culture, the culture of the profession, the disciplinary culture, the institutional culture, and individual cultural differences (Clark 1987).

Faculty socialization takes place in two general stages. The anticipatory stage includes undergraduate and especially graduate learning experiences. During graduate school, prospective faculty are intimately exposed to the norms of the professorate. At the conclusion of the graduate experience, prospective faculty have a solid understanding of what faculty life is like.

As graduate students leave their student status behind and are hired as new faculty, they enter the second stage of faculty socialization—the organizational stage. During this stage, faculty novices face a number of organizational challenges through which they often muddle by trial and error (Van Maanen and Schein 1979). For many new faculty, the first two years are characterized by loneliness and intellectual isolation, lack of collegial support, and heavy work loads and time constraints (Boice 1992).

While significant numbers of new faculty leave academe,

many find ways of coping with the stress of academic life and move from their novice status to more senior roles. Central to faculty advancement is the promotion and tenure process. From a cultural perspective, promotion and tenure practices serve as rites of passage to higher organizational status.

Although the early years of faculty life may be the most challenging, experienced faculty also face organizational obstacles which require ongoing learning. In this light, faculty socialization must be seen as a continuous process where even the most senior faculty must learn and relearn their roles within academic institutions.

In addition to being ongoing, socialization is bidirectional. Not only do people adapt to organizations, but organizations continually must adapt to their members. Viewing faculty socialization as bidirectional is crucial in creating diverse academic communities. While professors change to meet the demands of their academic institutions, colleges and universities must modify their structures to meet the needs of their diverse members. This means promotion and tenure rituals, as well as faculty development programs, must be continually reviewed.

What Are the Implications?

Organizational culture is complex, and individuals who are new to an organization will interpret that culture in different ways. Messages get confused and misinterpreted. Our contention is that the organizational messages related to succeeding as a faculty member—achieving tenure, for example—need to be clearly spelled out so that all organizational members have similar information from which to make decisions. In other words, faculty socialization should take place within the parameters of clearly articulated organizational goals and objectives.

The issues raised throughout this report relate to culture and commitment: What are the values to which academic organizations aspire? How do they communicate those values to organizational members? How do organizations affirm those values through various organizational structures? Our argument throughout this monograph is that coming to terms with faculty socialization holds answers to the preceding questions.

ADVISORY BOARD

CONSULTING EDITORS

Louis C. Attinasi, Jr.
University of Houston

Kimberly Brown
Portland State University

J. Kent Caruthers
MGT of America, Inc.

Elsa Kircher Cole
The University of Michigan

Jane F. Earley
Mankato State University

Walter H. Gmelch
Washington State University

James O. Hammons
University of Arkansas

Robert M. Hendrickson
The Pennsylvania State University

Barbara A. Lee
Rutgers University

Yvonna S. Lincoln
Texas A&M University

Robert J. Menges
Northwestern University

James L. Morrison
The University of North Carolina–Chapel Hill

Amaury Nora
University of Illinois–Chicago

Robert M. O'Neil
University of Virginia

Raymond V. Padilla
Arizona State University

Barbara S. Plakens
Iowa State University

William Rittenberg
Michigan State University

G. Jeremiah Ryan
Harford Community College

REVIEW PANEL

Charles Adams
University of Massachusetts–Amherst

Louis Albert
American Association for Higher Education

Richard Alfred
University of Michigan

Philip G. Altbach
State University of New York–Buffalo

Marilyn J. Amey
University of Kansas

Louis C. Attinasi, Jr.
University of Houston

Robert J. Barak
Iowa State Board of Regents

Alan Bayer
Virginia Polytechnic Institute and State University

John P. Bean
Indiana University

John M. Braxton
Vanderbilt University

Peter McE. Buchanan
Council for Advancement and
  Support of Education

John A. Centra
Syracuse University

Arthur W. Chickering
George Mason University

Shirley M. Clark
Oregon State System of Higher Education

Darrel A. Clowes
Virginia Polytechnic Institute and State University

John W. Creswell
University of Nebraska–Lincoln

Deborah DiCroce
Piedmont Virginia Community College

Richard Duran
University of California

Kenneth C. Green
University of Southern California

Edward R. Hines
Illinois State University

Marsha W. Krotseng
West Virginia State College and University Systems

George D. Kuh
Indiana University–Bloomington

Daniel T. Layzell
University of Wisconsin System

Meredith Ludwig
American Association of State Colleges and Universities

Mantha V. Mehallis
Florida Atlantic University

Robert J. Menges
Northwestern University

Toby Milton
Essex Community College

James R. Mingle
State Higher Education Executive Officers

Gary Rhoades
University of Arizona

G. Jeremiah Ryan
Harford Community College

Mary Ann Sagaria
Ohio State University

Daryl G. Smith
Claremont Graduate School

William Tierney
The Pennsylvania State University

Susan Twombly
University of Kansas

Harold Wechsler
University of Rochester

Michael J. Worth
The George Washington University

CONTENTS

FOREWORD

To be concerned with the quality of faculty performance is to be concerned with faculty socialization. Conversely, to understand how to maximize the faculty socialization process is to have a powerful tool to affect long-term institutional accomplishments. It is the socialization of an individual that makes up the sum total of values and norms that directs a person's daily responses and behavior patterns. The sum of all faculty socialization determines the culture of the organization and, ultimately, how well an organization functions.

The socialization process is most important to those occupations that function with little or no supervision. Members of these occupations, such as the professions represented by medical doctors, lawyers, and college faculty, are allowed to continue without the normal accountability of other occupations. This partially results from the belief that high standards of behavior have been instilled within each member of the profession through extensive schooling and reinforcement by the professional associations. Thus, most faculty receive very little direct supervision of their teaching and research.

However, it has been found that the socialization of faculty as graduate students changes over time. This was explained by John Creswell in *Faculty Research Performance: Lessons from the Sciences and Social Sciences*, an ASHE-ERIC Higher Education Report. Creswell noted that institutions often attempt to increase the research productivity of their programs by hiring graduates of top-ranking, highly productive graduate schools. These institutions assume that the new faculty will perform as they were socialized and do nothing to alter the institutional culture. The result is that within five years, the productivity of the new faculty has dropped to that of the level of the older faculty. The socialization process has been altered to the culture of the organization and not the opposite, as assumed when the new faculty were hired.

The mistake made by institutions is not the expectation that the academic output of the institution would be raised by hiring faculty from the highly productive graduate schools. The mistake was failing to pay attention to the socialization process that is at work within an institution's culture. It should be obvious—but it is not—that what is actually done or rewarded is what is valued. In other words, the socialization process is represented by that which receives constant reinforcement. Over time, this becomes the culture of the organization. It makes little difference what principles or values are articulated by the institutional leaders if these principles or values are not reinforced regularly. Examples of this are when an institution promotes teaching and learning as primary values but offers no training to the faculty and bases promotions on numbers of publications, or when staying on the cutting edge of knowledge is negatively reinforced by the elimination of travel monies to research conferences.

In this report by William G. Tierney, professor and senior scientist at The Pennsylvania State University, and Robert A. Rhoads, assistant professor of education and research associate at The Pennsylvania State University, faculty socialization is reviewed as an integral part of the culture of faculty life. While this culture is, in large part, that of the institution, it also consists of the culture of the nation, profession, discipline, and individual. The authors examine the socialization process and how it ultimately affects the success of faculty and their commitment and involvement with the institution.

A definition of insanity is to always do the same thing the same way but expect different results. If institutions wish to change their outcomes, they must be willing to examine the interrelated activities that make up the system that produces the outcomes. A major part of the system is the socialization process that directly determines the activities and responses of the faculty. Purposely defining what is desired from this process and then adjusting the process so it is more likely to produce that result will help to make significant, long-term, and permanent changes to the culture and outcomes of the institution.

Jonathan D. Fife
Series Editor, Professor of Higher Education Administration, and Director, ERIC Clearinghouse on Higher Education

ACKNOWLEDGMENTS

This publication was prepared partially with funding from
the Lilly Endowment. Part of our research efforts involved
interviewing tenure-track faculty. We appreciate the time they
spent with us and hope that the text accurately reflects some
of the struggles they face and ways to
overcome these obstacles.

CULTURE AND COMMITMENT

We live. And in living we believe, assert self, establish order around us, dominate others, or are dominated by them. Action flowing from meaning and intention weaves the fabric of social reality. . . . In this perspective, we may better understand organizations if we conceive them as being an invented reality (Greenfield 1980, p. 27).

Organizations exist as social constructions (Blumer 1969; Burke 1966; Mead 1934; Schutz 1970). To be sure, they exhibit formalized structures such as policies, rules, and decision-making committees, but just as importantly, they revolve around informal codes and expectations shared by organizational participants (Wanous 1992). These shared understandings and the formal and informal processes used to develop understanding and meaning account for what we refer to as organizational culture.

This sense of culture is captured best in the notion of "webs of significance."

Organizational culture shapes members' behavior; yet, at the same time, culture is shaped by the organizational actors. Culture is more than something that an organization has; instead, "culture is something an organization *is*" (Smircich 1983a, p. 347). This sense of culture is captured best in the notion of "webs of significance," where people simultaneously create and exist within culture (Geertz 1973). Individuals and groups are capable of changing a culture, but they also react to the culture's powerful mores and parameters.

Colleges and universities, as social institutions, each exhibit a unique organizational culture. Viewing higher education institutions in this manner has been well-documented in Kuh and Whitt's ASHE-ERIC report, *The Invisible Tapestry: Culture in American Colleges and Universities* (1988). Their work forms the starting point for this text. Kuh and Whitt noted a fundamental aspect of academic culture when they discussed faculty as one of three predominant subcultures situated within academe; the other two subcultures are students and administrators.

Our framework for this report is to focus on socialization as a cultural process that faculty become enmeshed within—and change, as well. We comment on the other subcultures of faculty life, such as that of the profession and discipline. We specifically focus on full-time faculty in our colleges and universities. We refer to the entire process as faculty socialization.

Our challenge is to define socialization in a "bidirectional" manner. By "bidirectional" we mean that socialization is a process that produces change in individuals as well as organizations. Socialization is not merely the analysis of how an individual changes to fit within the confines of a particular organization; we discuss socialization as a way for organizations to adapt and change to the diverse needs of the 21st century.

Significance of the Topic

During the 1980s and up to the present, higher education has come under a series of attacks. For some critics, American higher education has become too watered down, and students no longer are educated about the longstanding traditions associated with the American way of life and Western civilization (Bennett 1984; Kimball 1988). Relatedly, in the eyes of some educators and scholars, higher education has become too commonplace, and academic excellence has taken a backseat to accessibility (Association of American Colleges 1985; Commission for Educational Quality 1985).

Yet another criticism relates to the poor preparation of college graduates as they enter the labor market, ultimately reflected in our faltering economy (National Governors' Association 1986; Study Group 1984). Still others claim that higher education underscores the interests and values of dominant cultural groups and therefore neglects the experiences of the disenfranchised and underrepresented (Rossides 1984; Tierney 1992c; Weis 1985).

The position one takes with regard to the preceding arguments is contingent upon one's conception of higher education. When we examine how we think of higher learning, questions such as the following take on importance:

• Should higher education be the training ground for the American labor force?
• Should higher education provide students with an essential understanding of the Western tradition?
• Should higher education serve to legitimize diverse traditions and conceptions of life and human experience?
• Should higher education provide students with the essential critical values needed to participate as democratic citizens?

Throughout this report, we contend that faculty lie at the heart of the answers about such fundamental questions. Faculty sit on curricular and admissions committees, construct and teach courses, advise and counsel students, conduct research, and often serve as advisors to politicians and business leaders.

The role that faculty play in the formal and informal life of the institution is a key to understanding academic communities as cultures, since faculty are shaped by, and in turn, shape the institutional culture. The behaviors that faculty enact in institutional settings largely reflect their socialization experiences and the values and commitments of their institutions. This line of thinking follows the assumption that organizations socialize their members to adopt congruent values, beliefs, and attitudes. As noted, our purpose is not simply to develop a schema for efficient recruitment to and retention within the academy, for to do so overlooks the powerful ideas and beliefs individuals bring when they enter an organization.

As we elaborate, although faculty are employed by academic institutions, there are other significant influences beyond the institutional culture. Faculty have disciplinary affiliations that determine a great deal about their behavior. They face the influence of the profession of the professoriate. And the role of a faculty member in the United States is defined by our society's definition of what it means to be a professor.

To examine faculty life solely in relation to the academic institutions that hire faculty neglects significant other factors that play a role in faculty socialization, and the focus would be rather limited. If we are to respond adequately to the questions raised by recent critics of higher education, we must better understand the processes of culture and socialization in the academy so that our organizations are more receptive to new members' ideas, needs, and goals.

Faculty Diversity

While various debates about the purposes of higher education rage, few individuals argue that higher education should not strive toward equal opportunity. Yet, in spite of this apparent common ground, women and people of color remain underrepresented among the American professoriate. Women make up less than 30 percent of the professoriate and more than 50 percent of the U.S. population (Hamermesh 1992). People of color make up less than 12 percent of the professoriate ("Characteristics of Full-Time College Professors, 1987" 1992) and account for nearly 20 percent of the overall U.S. population.

Obviously, hiring and retaining women and people of color is key if we are to attain equal opportunity in higher education. A central aspect of achieving equal representation is understanding the socialization experiences of women and people of color, and in doing so we are able to consider socialization as an opportunity to enhance academic diversity. From this perspective, an organization's culture is not a monolith to which all individuals must uniformly respond.

A culture is open to different interpretations. One of the key challenges of understanding culture is discovering how we might adapt an organization's culture to multiple interpretations; at the same time, how do we develop shared understandings so that we enhance diversity rather than silence it?

Organizations as Cultures

In the late 1970s and early 1980s, organizational literature and research began to emphasize organizations as systems of shared meanings (Morgan, Frost, and Pondy 1983; Trice and Beyer 1984). Smircich noted that "the stability, or organization, of any group activity depends upon the existence of common modes of interpretation and shared understandings of experience" (1983b, p. 55). Relatedly, Greenfield argued that organizational analysis should focus on the *shared meanings* people have which define for them how to act within the organization (1973).

Other researchers concerned with understanding organizational culture have focused on the role that leaders play in shaping culture (Clark 1970; Pettigrew 1979; Pfeffer 1981; Pondy 1978; Schein 1985; Smircich and Morgan 1982; Smircich and Stubbart 1985). Related to much of the work on leadership is the notion that strong or congruent cultures lead to increased productivity or efficiency (Peters and Waterman 1982; Schwartz and Davis 1981; Wilkins and Ouchi 1983). Deal and Kennedy emphasized the role that values, heroes, rituals, and communication networks play in building strong corporate cultures (1982).

Additionally, various works have delineated strategies for unearthing organizational culture (Ouchi and Wilkins 1985; Trice and Beyer 1984). Wilkins, in discussing the "cultural audit," suggested that analysts examine the assumptions about employee work, reward, and punishment to better understand organizational culture (1983). Pettigrew emphasized the analysis of organizations over time as they move through various critical events or social dramas such as transitional phases in leadership turnover (1979). In sum, all of these analyses have worked from a social constructionist perspective to investigate organizations as cultures.

Colleges and Universities as Cultures

A number of scholars have examined various aspects of academic life by emphasizing cultural elements. A main focus of early cultural studies was understanding the student experience (Becker 1972; Feldman 1972; Feldman and Newcomb 1970; Lunsford 1963; Wallace 1966). More recent efforts in this area have been conducted by Moffatt, who explored student culture at Rutgers University (1989), and Holland and Eisenhart, who examined how peer culture—a "culture of romance"—influenced the college experiences of 24 women at two Southern universities (1990).

Identification of student subcultures and group associations has been a principal area of cultural investigation. Clark and Trow identified four student subcultures that defined general orientations exhibited by students: collegiate culture, vocational culture, academic culture, and non-conformist culture (1966). Other researchers have developed similar classifications and undertaken studies of those subcultures (Horowitz 1987).

Cultural research also has focused on faculty life. Becher examined the relationship between disciplinary affiliation and faculty behavior (1987, 1989). Clark explored the role that disciplines and institutions play in shaping faculty behavior (1987a). Freedman, in writing about academic culture and faculty development, described faculty culture as "a set of shared ways and views designed to make their [faculty] ills bearable and to contain their anxieties and uncertainties" (1979, p. 8). Since exploration of faculty life is a primary concern of this text, we devote section two to an extensive discussion of faculty culture.

While much of the early cultural research focused on specific cultural groups or subcultures, more recent work has examined academic institutions in a more holistic fashion, treating the institution itself as a culture—an organizational culture. This research has largely been built upon strategies employed by Clark (1963, 1970) and Riesman and Jencks (1962).

Tierney developed a framework for viewing colleges and universities as cultures emphasizing an understanding of the environment, mission, socialization, information, strategy, and leadership (1988a). Bensimon and Neumann (1992), Birnbaum (1988, 1992), Chaffee and Tierney (1988), Rhoads and Tierney (1992), and Tierney (1988b) discussed academic leadership in light of cultural theories. Tierney has adopted cultural frameworks to examine institutional mission and curricular decision making as well as the experiences of Native American students (1989, 1992c). Tierney and Rhoads (forthcoming) utilized a cultural framework in analyzing the higher education assessment movement. And finally, Bergquist identified four primary cultures at work in academe: a collegial culture that relates primarily to academic disciplines, a managerial culture that is identified with organization and administrative processes, a developmental culture that emphasizes the personal and professional growth of the college community, and a negotiating culture that focuses on the equitable distribution of organizational resources (1992).

Socialization from a Cultural Framework

Socialization is the process through which individuals acquire the values, attitudes, norms, knowledge, and skills needed to exist in a given society (Merton 1957). Organizational socialization is the same process at an organizational level. We analyze organizational socialization as a mutually adaptive process between the organization and the individual. Key aspects of organizational culture, such as ceremonies, rituals, and rites of passage, provide the necessary experiences by which values, beliefs, and attitudes are learned. However, as new members enter the academy, such rituals and ceremonies often need to be adapted or changed to meet the changed contexts that the initiates bring to the organization.

Socialization occurs through implicit and explicit actions. For faculty, implicit socialization may occur around the coffee machine, in the locker room, or at a wine and cheese party. Implicit socialization is difficult to observe and analyze, for it occurs spontaneously and unobtrusively. Explicit socialization involves clearly delineated cultural structures such as faculty development programs and the promotion and tenure process.

Our principal focus is to examine institutional processes that explicitly orient new faculty. Accordingly, we pay more attention to the socialization experiences of new faculty than senior faculty. We also expend more effort focusing on full-time faculty rather than adjunct faculty.

In the next two sections we explore culture and socialization in greater detail. In sections four, five, and six, we discuss the experiences of faculty as they move through multiple organizational roles and experiences. In the penultimate section, we discuss socialization as it relates to issues of diversity. The concluding section outlines institutional actions that might improve faculty socialization through the development of effective programs and activities that meet the multiple needs of faculty and enable the organization to adapt and change.

THE CULTURES OF FACULTY LIFE

*The many settings that make [the professorate] a patchwork
are tied by lines of affiliation that partly knit together the
profession's unraveling pattern. In this most varied profession, the tension between the many and the one is deeply
rooted in reality. Indeed, antithetical identities and commitments abound: the academic profession is haunted by
the play of contrary forces* (Clark 1987b, p. 371).

What are those "lines of affiliation," and how does one
become socialized to them? How do these different "identities" conflict and/or cohere with one another? In the section's first part, we identify the many-faceted cultures in which
faculty become socialized.

Faculty culture may be understood as a complex interplay
of symbolic meanings predicated on five sociological forces:
national, professional, disciplinary, individual, and institutional. In the United States, national influences primarily
derive from the overall culture of North American society and
form a backdrop for the other four forces. Professional influences derive from general notions related to what it means
to be a member of the professorate. Disciplinary influences,
of course, derive from one's disciplinary affiliation. Individual
forces relate to specific individual factors that may contribute
to significant differences in faculty experiences. Individual
influences include, for example, age, class, race, and gender.
Finally, institutional influences relate to the institutional culture with which a faculty member becomes associated.

As Clark noted, the complex fabric resulting from these
"antithetical identities and commitments" produces faculty
differences across a number of areas. To highlight these differences, in the section's second part we consider two areas
of conflict across faculty cultures: cosmopolitans versus locals,
and traditional paradigms versus emerging paradigms.

The Culture of the Nation

As any tourist knows, all countries have differences from that
of the visitor's. Behavior in some countries is more formal
than others: In one country, people are prompt; in another,
a concern for time may not be so evident. A belief in traditional family structures may play a crucial role in the actions
of citizens in one country and not in another. Such differences
are not merely national or individual stereotypes—"the British
are formal and North Americans are not"—but also highlight

---

the obvious: All cultures are unique and different. Such a point is especially important when one thinks about one's own culture, for often individuals think actions are unique only when they differ from one's own societal norms.

In the organizational worlds of the United States, for example, the organization's participants usually assume that appointments for meetings may be made weeks in advance and that a meeting begins on time. The North American researcher who visits a Latin American country and finds the concept of "time" to be dramatically different often is frustrated when meetings are not kept or they begin quite late. The simple point here is that cultural norms only hold for a specific culture, and how one acts and conceives of roles and organizations differs dramatically when we compare national attitudes about specific issues.

The concept of a faculty member in the United States is fundamentally different from that of a professor in an Islamic, Central American, or European nation. For example, in the Koran it is written that "the teacher is like the prophet Mohammed and you must respect him." Such a portrait of a faculty member is vastly different from those of us in the U.S. academy who generally do not enter classrooms with preordained religious rites of authority. Indeed, the separation between church and state in public institutions in the United States prohibits us from calling upon a religious text to invoke our wisdom. Similarly, the portrait of a woman as a professor in a college classroom may be considered common in the United States but provoke serious discussion in a fundamentalist country such as Iran.

In Central America, the concept of a faculty member is often of an individual who devotes part of his or her time to teaching students, but the individual holds another job as well. The idea that a professor is supposed to devote a significant portion of time to research often is absent. Similarly, concepts such as tenure, academic freedom, and institutional autonomy are dramatically different from such concepts in the United States. And finally, in Germany we see significant similarities to their U.S. counterparts in the types of work performed— but differences in power structures and lines of authority.

Consequently, individuals who become faculty in the United States are socialized to the role before they even begin graduate training. We are socialized to the role of a faculty member by our own experiences as undergraduate students, by the manner in which scholars conceptualize and write about North American higher education, and by what federal, state, and local governments and other constituencies such as private business expect of faculty.

To be sure, all cultures change. The national culture for faculty in the United States, Panama, or Germany, for example, is vastly different in 1994 than it was in 1934. But nonetheless, anyone who enters the academy today is well-socialized to what faculty are to do and how they are to comport themselves.

The Culture of the Profession

Influences related to the nature of the professorate as a profession are intertwined with the national identity. While one might argue that European universities had an academic profession in the 19th century, in many respects, the academic profession in the United States was in flux for all of the 19th and a large part of the 20th century. The evolution of the U.S. academic profession finally began to take shape around the end of World War II:

By the end of World War II, the components of the academic role had clearly emerged and crystallized into the highly differentiated model by which we recognize the professor today—teaching, research, student advisement, administration, institutional and public service (Finkelstein 1984, p. 29).

From what began as a small group of tutors instructing prospective ministers at Harvard College emerged a profession where instruction was only one facet of the overall role of the faculty member. We define profession as a form of an occupational community (Van Maanen and Barley 1984).

A profession is a group of people who engage in similar types of work, share common values and beliefs, and derive a similar sense of identity from their work. While faculty may be quite diverse across institutional type and discipline, they nonetheless perform many similar tasks, share common values and beliefs, and identify with one another as colleagues.

Faculty life is a distinct professional sphere governed by the norms of professional collegiality (Etzioni 1964). The academic profession exists through the members' own creativity and skills, and ultimately a member's contribution is judged

> *Faculty life is a distinct professional sphere governed by the norms of professional collegiality.*

by colleagues in the profession. Seen in this light, although obvious national differences exist, there also are commonalities that extend across borders. When someone notes that he or she is a faculty member, one gains a general picture of the life of that individual.

Academics create formal and informal bonds around common interests. The guild mentality of the academic profession frames faculty interests in a manner fundamentally different, for example, from that of someone in professional sports or someone who is in the dental profession. Again, individuals who decide to join the professorate—whether in the United States or Guatemala, in a private or public institution, or in the field of engineering or English literature—share preordained commonalities and are socialized accordingly.

Clark identified three prevailing ideologies across the profession (1987a). One ideology related to the "service of knowledge," where faculty described ideals about the investigation of new knowledge. Another ideology concerned the norms of academic honesty. Faculty indicate that a fundamental belief of their profession is a belief in intellectual integrity. As Clark noted, "In the academic lexicon, knowledge must be handled honestly, for otherwise it misinforms and deceives, is no longer valuable in itself, and certainly of no use to society" (p. 132). The third ideology related to the importance individuals placed on the idea of academic freedom.

With these first two faculty cultures—that of the nation and the profession—we observe potential conflicts and similarities on which we elaborate in the section's second part. Briefly, however, an individual raised in Spain will find that what the U.S. system of teaching and evaluation expects of a professor is quite different from what he or she was socialized to expect in Europe. A U.S. professor may experience surprise at the nature of classroom interactions when on sabbatical in Mexico.

And yet, certain constants hold firm. The discourse of the academy, how one relates to one's colleagues, and the manner in which one conducts his or her "work" often have greater similarities across countries than across professions. A French physicist and a Canadian chemist, for example, are socialized to share common work-related languages and customs more than would the French physicist with a countryman who is a banker.

The Culture of the Discipline

Although our hypothetical French physicist and Canadian chemist may share similarities, a French physicist would share an even greater sense of affiliation with a Chinese physicist, for they share the culture of a discipline. We may think of disciplines as any number of subgroupings within the profession, but disciplinary cultures also have unique aspects that socialize individuals in specific ways.

Some authors regard disciplines through a structural framework noting their appearance as organizational forms (Becher 1989). Others look more closely at disciplinary content and ask epistemological questions such as: What is its body of concepts? What are its methods? What are its fundamental aims? (Toulmin 1972). Still others focus on the content and the structural qualities of disciplines. For example, Ladd and Lipset (1975) described a discipline as:

> *a unit of association in which faculty members spend large portions of their professional lives. These associations are personal. A professor will often know members of his field at universities across the country better than he will know most people in other departments at his own university. But his associations within his field are with bodies of ideas, interests, norms and values, and professional styles as well* (p. 56).

In understanding what constitutes a discipline, then, it is prudent to include both structural and epistemological qualities.

Over a quarter of a century ago Snow elaborated the notion that the academic world consisted principally of two cultures: the worlds of the sciences and of the humanities (1959). In a more recent analysis of faculty culture, we find that the cultural worlds of the disciplines have exploded so that faculty no longer may be divided easily into one of two groups (Becher 1989). Interestingly, the idea of a discipline has become more structured and more diffuse.

New epistemological areas of knowledge such as biochemistry and women's studies have arisen, and at the same time, the structures of disciplines have become more rigid and defined so that one publishes in specialized journals and attends conferences on specialized topics. However, interdisciplinary analysis also has come of age; we now find literary critics who use anthropological models and courses that combine scientific with historical texts.

Socialization to the discipline normally begins formally in graduate school, although one starts to be socialized to a discipline as an undergraduate who majors in an area. Graduate students learn to master language specific to their field of study, read journals germane to that area, and discover conferences that they are advised to attend either to present a paper, meet colleagues, or interview for a job. As we shall see in section five, disciplinary socialization continues as tenure-track faculty struggle to make presentations and publish in refereed journals pertinent to their disciplinary focus.

Research also has found that significant differences related to personal characteristics and attitudes exist across disciplines. For example, social science faculty are the most politically liberal faculty, whereas the least liberal are those faculty in applied professional careers. "Each discipline," noted Bowen and Schuster, "attracts individuals of particular talents and interests, and the experience of working in each field places its mark on their personalities" (1986, p. 49). We find, then, yet another cultural cross-current where one's background may attract or repel an individual toward a disciplinary culture.

Finally, Kuh and Whitt have argued, "The culture of the discipline is the primary source of faculty identity and expertise and typically engenders stronger bonds than those developed with the institution of employment, particularly in large universities" (1988, p. 77). This point is important to keep in mind as we begin to deal more specifically with faculty socialization, for if a discipline plays the preeminent role in faculty socialization, then questions need to be raised about what institutions will be able to accomplish with regard to shaping faculty culture.

Culture and the Individual

Another significant factor in shaping faculty culture is individual differences that relate to large categories such as race, class, gender, sexual orientation, or other more microscopic qualities a person may bring to his or her position (Dunn, Seff, and Rouse forthcoming). With regard to social categories, we know, for example, that American Indians make up .7 percent of the professorate, Asian Americans 4.2 percent, African-Americans 3.2 percent, and Hispanics 2.3 percent. Women account for approximately 27.3 percent of the total full-time faculty ("Characteristics of Full-Time College Professors" 1992). While these figures lag behind national figures, they nonetheless highlight the significance that diverse groups play in shaping faculty culture. That is, social characteristics such as gender have a significant impact on how one is socialized to a discipline or organization.

Individuals and social groups experience faculty life in unique ways. An African-American presumably experiences academe in a manner different from a Hispanic or Asian American. Men's experiences differ from women's. Since we devote section seven to the issue of faculty diversity and the unique challenges of women and people of color, we save that discussion for later. Suffice to say for now that a number of scholars have documented the experiences of faculty from diverse cultural groups, and that academe in general has not done a good job socializing individuals to the organization and adapting the organization to diverse groups of people (Aisenberg and Harrington 1988; Bernard 1964; Luz Reyes and Halcon 1991; McKay 1983; Moore and Wagstaff 1974; Olivas 1988; Simeone 1987; Tierney 1992a; Tierney and Rhoads 1993).

The Culture of the Institution
All of these faculty cultures are enacted within the organization's culture. The national, professional, disciplinary, and individual influences of a faculty member get played out on the terrain of the college or university. And further, that terrain is also a faculty culture.

The culture of an organization is determined by the manner in which the institution communicates meaning, the purpose of that meaning, and how that meaning is to be interpreted. Institutional parameters such as size and type are obviously a major force in shaping the general orientation of faculty work (Blau 1973; Caplow and McGee 1958). However, differences in an organization's mission, how leadership is demonstrated, and the symbols the organization uses to communicate among members also affect the daily lives of faculty members.

Within the culture of an organization is where the conflicts with the other cultures may be seen most clearly. How might we enable collegiate organizations to more successfully orchestrate the manifold cultures which shape faculty life? Such work involves an understanding of these faculty cultures, the dynamics of the organization's culture, and socialization.

TABLE 1

Summary of Faculty Cultures

FACULTY	CHARACTERISTIC
National Culture	Varies by country/society (United States, Brazil, Panama)
Professional Culture	Varies by occupation (doctor, police officer, teacher)
Disciplinary Culture	Varies by area of study (physics, sociology, women's studies, engineering)
Institutional Culture	Varies by institution based on factors such as type, size, location, public vs. private
Individual Cultural Differences	Varies by individual qualities (race, age, gender, sexual orientation, physical disability)

Faculty Commitments

As noted, one faculty culture may overlap, conflict, or be entirely different from another. The faculty member must work out these conflicts and trade-offs on a daily basis. At times, of course, trade-offs and compromises are impossible; conflict for an individual changes from merely becoming a nuisance to the need to find another job. Nevertheless, the strength of one's socialization into the discipline may affect whether the individual identifies predominantly with the institution or the discipline. Likewise, institutional type may play a major role in a faculty member's identification with the discipline or the institution.

Other behaviors such as one's commitment to advising, university outreach, or service also are shaped by the intersection of these complex cultural forces. We offer two examples that highlight faculty differences and are contingent upon the intersection of cultural forces: commitment to the institution (locals) or to the discipline (cosmopolitans) and commitment to traditional or emerging paradigms.

Cosmopolitans and locals

Various strategies have been used to delineate faculty life. As long ago as 1957, faculty were described in terms of cosmopolitans and locals (Gouldner 1957a, 1957b). Cosmopolitans are "those low on loyalty to the employing organization, high on commitment to specialized role skills, and likely to use an outer reference group orientation" (p. 290). Locals, on the other hand, are "those high on loyalty to the employing organization, low on commitment to specialized role skills, and likely to use an inner reference group orientation" (p. 290). In terms of the professorate, those faculty more committed to their discipline than to the institution are described as cosmopolitans, whereas faculty committed to the institution are described as locals.

Obviously, the distinction between cosmopolitan and local speaks to the culture of the discipline and organization (Becher 1987; Blau 1973; Clark 1987a; Freedman 1979). One of the paradoxes of U.S. graduate education is that we train and socialize the vast majority of those who will become faculty in research institutions, and then that vast majority finds itself in organizations where the culture does not reward research in a manner akin to the research university.

An individual faces a dysfunctional work life where he or she has been socialized to conduct research but finds there is virtually no time to do so because of the teaching load. Similarly, an individual who values teaching may feel undervalued at an institution where only research is rewarded.

Traditional paradigms and emerging paradigms

In recent years, much debate has surfaced over issues related to science, in general, and theory and method, in particular. These debates tend to revolve around emerging interpretations of science versus more traditional research paradigms. While at one time scientific practice might have had clearly identifiable norms (Merton 1973), such an argument is more difficult to make today (Braxton 1986; Hackett 1990).

Kuhn was one of the first to call attention to the changing face of scientific and scholarly work when he highlighted the "paradigm revolution" (1970). Others have described the methods employed by many of today's scholars as "blurred genres" (Geertz 1983). This trend in science and theory has had implications for how faculty go about conducting research, especially in the social sciences. A variety of methodologies and theories have been spawned by this general critique of traditional science. Thus, one of the significant issues for understanding key aspects of faculty culture relates to the professor's orientation toward more traditional scientific methods or emerging paradigms.

The way scholars conceive of knowledge relates to the types of inquiries that may be conducted. Traditionally, knowledge has been situated within academic disciplines. Recently, however, some of the bonds that frame the academic disciplines have begun to crack. "Today, more than at any time in recent memory," comments Ernest Boyer, "researchers feel the need to move beyond traditional disciplinary boundaries, communicate with colleagues in other fields, and discover patterns that connect" (1990, p. 20). The changing structure of the disciplinary culture calls into question what it means to be a member of a national culture and the structure in which organizational cultures place knowledge. That is, in a world where disciplinary culture now incorporates interdisciplinary thought, traditional departments may no longer suffice.

At a time when knowledge and research findings may be transmitted across the world in a matter of seconds, the fragmentation and difference of national cultures may lessen. At the same time, in those countries that do not have the resources to develop the necessary telecommunications networks, national and disciplinary cultures may be in ever greater conflict. Conversely, at a stage in the United States where calls for closer relationships between academe and society are commonplace, what it means to be a member of the profession may undergo change. This, in turn, will affect organizational rewards and incentives and one's relationship to a discipline.

Summary

We have examined the complex makeup of faculty lives by discussing these cultural forces: the academic discipline, the profession of the professorate, the institution, and individual difference all framed by the larger influence of the national culture of American society. The influences weave a fabric which results in faculty differences and similarities evidenced across a number of orientations or faculty commitments. While there are many points of intersection, we have considered two: commitment to the institution (locals) or to the discipline (cosmopolitans) and commitment to disciplinary work or interdisciplinary work.

The importance of understanding faculty culture is preeminent if we are to adequately examine the socialization of faculty. While we have noted that the institution is only one of the key forces that shape faculty culture and behavior, it nonetheless plays a critical role in the socialization of faculty. We now consider the specifics of organizational socialization and relate the discussion to faculty socialization.

CONCEPTUALIZING FACULTY SOCIALIZATION

*The self is not so much a substance as a process in which
the conversation of gestures has been internalized within
an organic form. This process does not exist for itself, but
is simply a phase of the whole social organization of which
the individual is a part* (Mead 1934, p. 178).

Socialization is a concept that has concerned social scientists
throughout the 20th century. For some, socialization is a
means for achieving a sense of solidarity by the institution-
alization of shared values (Merton 1957; Parsons and Shils
1951). For others, socialization is a means for reproducing
the mores of the dominant culture (Bourdieu 1977). Some
theorists have investigated socialization as a common need
across all cultures (Levi-Strauss 1963), and others have considered the interaction between the individual psyche and
the social organization (Goffman 1959, 1967; Mead 1934).

Many anthropologists have thought of some forms of socialization as a ritualized situation (Turner 1977). Van Gennep,
for example, studied "rites of passage" that socialized individuals to the larger society (1960). These rituals were
designed to move individuals from one developmental stage
to another. The most obvious form of such rituals were those
used for adolescents who were to become adults. Educational
anthropologists (Spindler and Spindler 1989) and social
scientists (McLaren 1986; Tinto 1987) also have considered
how students become socialized to society through the educational organization.

We view socialization as a ritualized process that involves
the transmission of culture. In what follows, we elaborate on
our definition of organizational socialization and then delineate the stages in which faculty become involved.

*As a process,
socialization
is ongoing,
although it
occurs most
clearly when
new recruits
enter the
organization.*

Organizational Socialization Defined

Organizational socialization is a cultural process that involves
the exchange of patterns of thought and action. As a process,
socialization is ongoing, although it occurs most clearly when
new recruits enter the organization. For new members, organizational socialization is "the process of 'learning the ropes,'
the process of being trained, the process of being taught what
is important in an organization" (Schein 1968, p. 2). And yet,
as a process, the organization's members always are involved
in socialization.

A new leader, for example, enters the institution with a significantly different vision about the organization, and those in the organization perhaps may have to reframe previously held beliefs. An individual spends a year away from the organization on a sabbatical, and upon return, has a different way of seeing the institution. And obviously, any long-term member of an organization will point out how different the organization is today than when he or she first entered. A cultural view of organizations highlights change rather than stasis. We need to consider socialization from a similar viewpoint.

Socialization's purpose is twofold. On one hand, "One of the important functions of organizational socialization is to build commitment and loyalty to the organization" (Schein 1968, p. 7). Individuals learn about the organization's culture. On the other hand, since an organization's culture is interpretive and dynamic, as new members enter the institution it is resocialized. We are suggesting that since an organization's culture exists as the product of social relations, as new members engage the organization they are able to change it (Tierney 1992b).

In this regard, our interpretation of faculty socialization differs from traditional notions that have stressed a one-directional process (Baldwin 1979; Baldwin and Blackburn 1981; Blackburn 1985). In today's diverse society an organization's participants need to re-think how faculty become enmeshed within an organizational setting. This point is crucial to bear in mind as individuals consider groups such as women or African-Americans, since they have been excluded and/or underrepresented in academe. Similarly, as young faculty enter an institution with an interdisciplinary orientation, the organization needs to respond in ways different from the past. How might the organization be transformed as significant cadres of faculty enter with different perspectives and orientations?

We have pointed out how a leader such as a college president may play a key role in reorienting the organization's culture, and hence, socialization. Long-term members also play a significant role in socializing the young. The point stressed here is that as an interpretive site of negotiation, an organization's culture has the potential to undergo change in any number of different manners due to the multiplicity of voices that exist. Socialization is a highly charged process, where different individuals and groups come together to define organizational beliefs and attitudes. Rather than simply a sense of events, it is an ongoing process which involves virtually all organizational actors.

Faculty Socialization
A new professor enters a postsecondary institution and in one way or another becomes accustomed to the organization's norms. At some institutions, faculty dress formally, while at other institutions, faculty will be found in shorts and sneakers. At one institution, faculty are expected to be in their offices a great deal of time, while at another locale, faculty offices are little more than way stations between classes. Some institutions value research and others teaching. How do individuals come to learn about these norms, and how do these norms change? Faculty socialization is one area that provides clues.

Faculty socialization is a process with two stages: the anticipatory stage and the organizational stage. Anticipatory socialization occurs largely during graduate school. The organizational stage involves initial entry and then role continuance. The organizational stage occurs when a faculty member enters the institution for the first time and comes into contact with the institutional culture. The contact between the prospective faculty member and the institutional culture occurs initially during the recruitment and selection process (Wanous 1992).

Stage One: Anticipatory Socialization
The first step in organizational socialization involves anticipatory learning on the part of the potential recruit (Van Maanen 1976, 1983). Anticipatory socialization pertains to how non-members take on the attitudes, actions, and values of the group to which they aspire.

Anticipatory socialization serves three functions: "For the individual who adopts the values of a group to which he [she] aspires but does not belong, the orientation may serve the twin functions of aiding his [her] rise into that group and of easing his [her] adjustment after he [she] has become a part of it" (Merton 1957, p. 265). At the same time, new members also begin to reframe the group to which they will belong.

During graduate training, for example, students anticipate the types of roles and behaviors they must enact to succeed as faculty members. Graduate training is where students begin to acquire the values, norms, attitudes, and beliefs associated with their discipline and with the profession at large. "As

young scholars work with professors, they observe and internalize the norms of behavior for research as well as supporting mechanisms such as peer review and academic freedom" (Anderson and Seashore-Louis 1991, p. 63).

At the same time, graduate students choose dissertation topics and areas of study that may help dramatically reorient a discipline. Native American Studies and Women's Studies are but two examples that benefited by the backgrounds of the "new recruits." These individuals interacted with the "norms" by reconfiguring them. And too, the manner in which work is done also changes as the backgrounds of these recruits change.

In examining the training of medical students, Becker et al. argued that students create their own culture which aids them in surviving medical school (1961). This culture is not necessarily geared toward adopting the future values and attitudes associated with becoming a doctor but is more short term in its orientation. They described student culture as "the working out in practice of the perspectives from which the students view their day-to-day problems in relation to their long-term goals. The perspectives, themselves collectively developed, are organizations of ideas and actions" (p. 435).

However, the development of a student culture takes place within an organizational context in which various problems, dilemmas, and situations are placed before the medical students by faculty, residents, and interns. While the short-term implications of the organizational context may be the emergence of a student culture geared toward survival, there also are significant long-term effects. The general set of perspectives that Becker and others highlight as a by-product of medical training is one facet of anticipatory socialization.

For aspiring faculty, graduate training, then, serves as a significant force in socializing students into the roles and expectations associated with faculty life. How one interacts with students and colleagues, the lifestyle one leads, and the journals, conferences, and books that one reads initially are learned from mentors and peers in graduate school.

These initial socializing experiences that new faculty bring to an institution may not necessarily match the culture of their new organization. A biologist trained at Harvard to value research may experience a mismatch of expectations if she arrives at a state college without research facilities. A United States historian who is trained to use a seminar style in teaching may be surprised if, for one reason or another, his career begins in an Islamic university that exclusively employs the lecture.

Our point is straightforward: Socialization begins prior to an individual's first day of employment. The individual learns what it means to be a member of a profession and discipline during one's training, and this learning may be at odds with what he or she ultimately finds. Since human beings constantly try to make sense of the culture, the events and messages that are provided during one's initial interaction with an institution send potent symbols. A university may not be able to alter the students' graduate school socialization, but it has vast discretion over institutional structures that frame the organizational experience.

Stage Two: Organizational Socialization

The organizational stage has two phases: initial entry and role continuance. The entry phase involves interactions that might occur during the recruitment and selection process as well as the early period of organizational learning that occurs as soon as the individual begins employment.

The role continuance phase begins after the individual is situated in the organization. The organizational stage is initially framed by activities that occurred during the anticipatory socialization of the recruit that has helped shape understandings and responses to the task demands and performance requirements (Van Maanen 1983).

When anticipatory socialization for an individual is consistent with that of the organization's culture, then the recruit will experience socialization processes which affirm the individual qualities brought to the organization. On the other hand, if the values, beliefs, and norms brought by a recruit are seen as inconsistent with the cultural ethos of the institution, then the socialization experience will be more transformative in nature: The organization will try to modify an individual's qualities.

In terms of faculty socialization, transformative processes occur when a faculty member with a research orientation enters an institutional setting where teaching takes precedence, or conversely, when a new faculty member is hired at a research university but enters with a teaching orientation. Obviously, to a certain degree, everyone goes through transformations upon entering an organization. Organizational leaders need to be conscious of what kinds of transformations are important and necessary, and what kinds are trivial.

If recruits survive the initial entry process and the experiences that go along with being a "novice," they gradually move to a role continuance phase (Corcoran and Clark 1984). Junior faculty must master the necessary academic and cultural skills to attain tenure. Tenured faculty need to become socialized to the responsibilities of academic leadership, and so on. Hence, organizational socialization is a two-phase process. Recruits first enter an organization and begin to "learn the ropes" during the initial years of their academic life and then expand their organizational role.

Most often, organizational socialization occurs informally and haphazardly. A new faculty member arrives on campus and learns from other faculty members about the in's and out's of the environment. Younger faculty learn how to act in meetings from the behavior of older colleagues. An assistant professor hears senior faculty speak constantly about the importance of publications and never mention participation in university service, so she declines to attend the faculty senate.

Although informal organizational socialization will always occur, one of the key purposes of this text is to suggest that an organization's participants need to consider more consciously how to socialize individuals to the organization's culture. When individuals do not make the organization's culture explicit to new members, they are assuming that individuals all interpret the institution's symbolic life in the same way. Our suggestion is to consider strategies that socialize the organization's participants not simply to unquestioned norms, but also to consider what those norms are and how they might need to be changed with the inclusion of new groups of faculty. Such a process means that all individuals are involved in ongoing organizational socialization and learning.

Dimensions of Organizational Socialization
Van Maanen and Schein have proposed "tactical strategies" for understanding organizational socialization (1979). By tactical, they refer to the ways that "the experiences of individuals in transition from one role to another are structured for them by others in the organization" (p. 232). The dimensions of organizational socialization are: 1) collective versus indi-

vidual; 2) formal versus informal; 3) sequential versus random; 4) fixed versus variable; 5) serial versus disjunctive; and 6) investiture versus divestiture.

Collective vs. individual

Collective socialization refers to forming a group of recruits who face a common set of experiences together. Examples of this type of socialization include soldiers during boot camp, students during graduate school, or a significant number of tenure-track faculty in a particular school or college. Distinctive colleges such as Reed College in Oregon, Deep Springs College in California, or Hampshire College in Massachusetts are examples of a unitary framework for organizational socialization, since their culture is unitary and collective as opposed, for example, to large public institutions that have a more disparate culture.

Individual socialization refers to processing new members in an isolated and singular manner. Individual socialization more aptly describes the experiences of faculty in the vast majority of colleges and universities. Faculty generally are hired on a departmental or divisional basis with little coordination across organizational boundaries. Faculty experiences throughout their tenure are generally individualized experiences. Some institutions provide campuswide orientation and/or development programs, but these are, for the most part, short-term experiences.

Formal vs. informal

A second tactical dimension of organizational socialization pertains to whether the socialization experiences are formal or informal. Formal socialization relates to those experiences where the recruit is separated from other regular members of the organization while participating in a series of specifically designed activities. Formal socialization is to what we referred previously as a rite of passage; the initiate undergoes a structured experience to pass to a new stage—complete with a new organizational status.

Informal socialization relates to more laissez-faire experiences where the norms of the organization are learned through trial and error. Faculty socialization, generally, is most typically a "sink or swim" proposition and is more informal than formal. Van Maanen and Schein elaborate on informal socialization (1979).

*Learning through experience in the informal socialization
mode . . . place recruits in the position where they must
select their own socialization agents. The value of this mode
to the newcomer is then determined largely by the relevant
knowledge possessed by an agent and, of course, the agent's
ability to transfer such knowledge* (p. 238).

If we agree that faculty socialization takes place to a significant
degree through an informal process, then it logically follows
that at a minimum, new faculty need experienced and caring
mentors.

Random vs. sequential

Another tactical dimension relates to random versus sequential socialization. Random socialization pertains to a progres-
sion of unclear or ambiguous steps which lead to a target goal
or role. While the goal may be clear, how to achieve the goal
is unclear. Sequential socialization involves discrete and
identifiable steps for achieving an organizational role. This
type of socialization is more ordered and clear and typically
falls in line with formal and collective socialization processes.

Random socialization describes processes associated with
faculty evidenced by the tremendous stress, ambiguity, and
confusion faculty experience in pursuit of promotion and tenure. One is never sure how much to write, how good a
teacher to be, or what to do in terms of public service to attain
promotion or tenure. Although the target may be clear, the
process to achieve it is not. Some aspects of the promotion
process in the U.S. military may be seen as examples of
sequential socialization in that certain tests must be taken and
passed, specific skills must be acquired, and certain educational levels must be attained before a soldier can be pro-
moted to the next level.

Fixed vs. variable

Fixed versus variable socialization processes refer to whether
the timetable related to moving through different organizational roles is fixed (precisely spelled out) or variable (vague
and unclear). An example of fixed socialization is high school
graduation—12 years of successful schooling typically moves
someone to a new status as a high school graduate. Obtaining
the Ph.D., however, might be considered a type of variable
socialization, in that the process involves rites of passage that

frequently are unclear and variable across individuals based on their own level of ability or accomplishment.

Usually, transitions from one role to another for faculty are a mixture of fixed and variable processes. The passage from novice through the promotion and tenure process is relatively fixed—usually six years. The role continuance that occurs when a person passes from an associate professor to a full professor is more an individualistic time frame and thus much more variable.

Serial vs. disjunctive

Serial socialization refers to the planned training of an individual by a senior member. A disjunctive socialization process is one where no role models are available for the organizational newcomer. An untenured faculty member might be trained by a tenured professor, or a new department chair might learn from someone who has been a chair for a considerable time.

For faculty, having experienced role models seems critically important. At a minimum, individuals need peer support. This is problematic for underrepresented groups, since issues related to gender, race, and sexual orientation may make the mentoring process more difficult.

Investiture vs. divestiture

The final dimension relates to investiture versus divestiture socialization processes, which we discuss in terms of an affirming versus a transforming socialization experience. Investiture (more affirming) concerns the welcoming of the recruit's anticipatory socialization experiences and individual characteristics, whereas divestiture (more transforming) involves stripping away those personal characteristics seen as incompatible with the organizational ethos.

When newcomers take their first faculty position, two generalized institutional patterns may result. On one hand, the institution encourages and reinforces those experiences learned in graduate school (investiture). On the other hand, institutional gatekeepers might adopt a transformative stance and attempt to restructure the new member's values, norms, and beliefs (divestiture). Investiture versus divestiture processes may be enacted at the same time, but with regard to different aspects of the novice's orientation.

One is never sure how much to write, how good a teacher to be, or what to do in terms of public service to attain promotion or tenure.

Subsequently, a new faculty member who did not attain tenure at a research university may be hired by a teaching-oriented institution and the faculty member's values, norms, and beliefs associated with the research function may need to be modified. The college may adopt a transformative stance toward the new faculty member's view of the importance of research. At the same time, this new member may place great value on the teaching role, and the institution likely would affirm this quality. Unfortunately, as we have noted, few real institutional mechanisms are enacted in any kind of formalized way. Instead, qualities of new faculty are affirmed or transformed through informal mechanisms that are, for the most part, imprecise and haphazard.

Another difficulty related to faculty socialization and the notions of investiture versus divestiture socialization is the fact that dominant norms, values, and beliefs tend to get reproduced. Logically, it follows that if an institution values certain characteristics, it will look for those qualities in new recruits. However, members of underrepresented groups may bring personal characteristics and anticipatory experiences that are incongruent with some of the dominant values of the organization, and the organization may enact transformative processes to modify the new recruit.

Summary

During the anticipatory stage of graduate school, the prospective faculty member's experience is shaped by four cultural influences that produce a general orientation. These cultural forces relate to disciplinary influences, professional influences, individual factors, and influences that derive from society. In the second stage of faculty socialization, the recruit begins to learn about an organization's culture, which becomes the fifth cultural force in shaping the faculty member's occupational life (see Figure 1 for a visual summary of faculty socialization).

During stage two, the newly hired faculty member arrives at an institution and must learn about the organization's culture while at the same time he or she continues to be shaped by the four other cultural influences. Organizational socialization has two phases: initial entry and role continuance. The entry phase moves the individual from the role of outsider to novice. The role continuance phase relates to the continuing relationship between the institution and the faculty member. Essential to understanding this phase in academe is the promotion and tenure process.

FIGURE 1

Faculty Socialization

STAGE ONE Anticipatory	STAGE TWO Organizational Socialization
Four Cultural Influences 1. National Culture 2. Professional Culture 3. Disciplinary Culture 4. Individual Cultural Differences	**Five Cultural Influences** 1. National Culture 2. Professional Culture 3. Disciplinary Culture 4. Individual Cultural Differences 5. Institutional Culture

Phase One | Phase Two

| Entry | Role Continuance |

Dimensions of Faculty Socialization
1. Collective . . . . Individual
(group vs. singular)
2. Formal . . . . Informal
(isolated from organizational members or interwoven with organizational members)
3. Random . . . . Sequential
(unclear and ambiguous vs. ordered steps)
4. Fixed . . . . Variable
(specific timetable vs. no timetable)
5. Serial . . . . Disjunctive
(lead by role models vs. no role models)
6. Investiture . . . . Divestiture
(affirming of individual characteristics to transforming individual characteristics)

THE FACULTY MEMBER AS NOVICE

Academic life is a mad hazard (Weber 1919, p. 133).

The focus of this section is on the interaction between the new faculty member and the institution as the employing organization. This initial entry into the ranks of the professorate marks the beginning of the organizational socialization process. In describing the faculty member as a novice, we refer principally to newly hired assistant professors in their first years of faculty work. Although socialization has a cumulative effect where an individual's experiences within organizations build on each other, organizational participants must pay particular attention to those initial experiences that occur for an individual within an organization.

Over the last decade, for example, research has shown how important the first-year experience is for college students. More students depart during their initial year than in subsequent years. Patterns of study, interaction, and attitudes are set more clearly in the first year than in any other. We are suggesting that the same patterns also occur in faculty roles (Dunn, Seff, and Rouse forthcoming). Of consequence, it behooves academic leaders to better understand the initial socializing experiences of the new recruit so that, as with the first-year experience for college students, programs of support might be implemented.

We focus on two primary aspects of early organizational entry: (1) the recruitment and selection process as a means of organizational socialization and (2) the experiences of new hires as they become socialized into their roles as faculty. While we recognize that much of what drives the early socialization of faculty is, in fact, the promotion and tenure process, we save that discussion for the following section, since it is the central socializing ritual of academic life.

Recruitment and Selection

The recruitment and selection process marks the first formal communication between the prospective faculty member and the organization. The job description that an institution advertises tells a prospective employee something about the values of the institution. Evergreen State College in Washington, for example, requires all applicants to submit a statement about their philosophy of education and teaching. Other institutions ask applicants to submit writing samples. Still other institutions ask individuals to teach a class or present a paper. Some applications must be submitted to the dean of the college and others to the chair of the search committee. To the neophyte, these are initial cultural clues about what the institution values and how it is structured.

Interviews and the experience that candidates have when they visit campus provide additional information (Waggaman 1983.). An institution where the president or dean interviews a candidate offers one kind of information, and an interview where senior faculty are too busy to speak with a candidate provides another kind of information. An interview where a candidate must make a formal presentation about a research topic highlights an institution's concern for research, whereas the absence of such a discussion sends another signal.

In general, at the center of the recruitment and selection process is the academic department, where much of the decision making regarding new faculty tends to reside (McHenry 1977). Academic departments not only represent concerns related to the organization, but additionally, departments usually are aligned with a discipline. The role of the discipline in the recruitment and selection process, as well as its influence on the experiences of the new recruit, highlight the powerful and ongoing influence of the disciplinary culture.

From a rational perspective of the organization, the primary goal of recruitment and selection is to match the departmental/organizational needs and interests with the talents, skills, and interests of the prospective faculty member. The same might be said of the prospective faculty member (Wanous 1992), although in tight job markets candidates often initially are thankful to have located a job. A cultural analysis of recruitment and selection, however, offers a different interpretation.

Although the process certainly involves finding the right "fit" between organization and candidate, the kind of matches that are involved relate primarily to the cultures of faculty life. The culture of the institution may differ from what an individual has learned from the culture of the discipline or nation. The importance of research and teaching and how they function are the most obvious examples where cultural differences will occur. Similarly, the culture of an institution that is primarily white or male may differ dramatically from the cultural background of an individual who is neither male nor white.

A serious problem may result when a new faculty member oriented toward a disciplinary culture of research is hired at a teaching-oriented institution (Braskamp, Fowler, and Ory

1984). Likewise, problems may arise when the opposite occurs: when a faculty member with a teaching orientation is hired, only to discover that research is critical. Similarly, implicit messages may be sent that someone does not "fit" the culture of the organization, when in reality the issue is that the individual is culturally different from the norms of the institution.

The challenge for the institution is twofold. First, the institution's participants need to be reflective about the explicit values of the culture. If the institution, for example, believes that teaching is of paramount importance, then clear signals need to be sent to the candidate immediately about what is expected of him or her. Second, the institution's participants need to understand how the implicit mechanisms of the organization's culture operate, so that they might understand how to make new faculty members welcome. Language, events, and interactions all are loaded with symbolic meaning. If the institution honors diversity, then it needs to consider how organizational symbols privilege some and silence others.

Further, institutions frequently are in the process of change, in which they try to reform the organizational culture by becoming more diverse or increasing the importance of teaching, for example. One way of producing organizational change is to bring in new people with different values and orientations. Hiring new faculty represents an opportune time to reshape the organization, but these individuals also need the support to sustain change. For example, a college dean who gives prominence to teaching in a specific college when the university does not do so will create problems for the novice who listens to the dean but finds out at promotion and tenure that the university actually rewards research.

The Experiences of New Faculty
Once a candidate has been chosen and hired, the new faculty member enters an experience fraught with unique problems and concerns. "The new professor's major concern is competence. . . . This entry period is a time of intense pressure and considerable growth" (Baldwin 1990, p. 31).

Newcomers to academe face a number of organizational challenges. Frequently, they either are tested informally or formally about their abilities, motives, and values before being granted inclusionary rights which permit them (1) to share organizational secrets; (2) to separate the rhetoric used with outsiders in describing the institution from the rhetoric used by insiders to communicate with one another; and (3) to understand the unofficial, yet recognized, norms associated with the actual work occurring and the moral conduct expected of people in specific organizational segments (Van Maanen and Schein 1979).

In many ways, the early years of faculty life are a period of disillusionment and adjustment (Olsen and Sorcinelli 1992; Sorcinelli 1992). In a study of new faculty at a large regional university, Boice reported consistent feelings of loneliness and intellectual understimulation (1991a, 1992). Relatedly, Boice described general complaints on the part of new faculty about lack of collegiality. A number of researchers noted findings related to time pressures described by new faculty (Mager and Myers 1982; Sorcinelli 1988, 1992; van der Bogert 1991). Still others have highlighted the difficulty in learning the informal aspects of organizational culture (Baldwin 1979; Mager and Myers 1982).

Loneliness and intellectual isolation
Based on extensive interviews conducted with four successive new faculty cohorts, Boice identified feelings of loneliness and isolation as one of the more significant problems faced by new faculty (1991a, 1992). The long hours required of professorial work lie at the heart of the loneliness and isolation new faculty experience. Most faculty novices agree that the first year is a difficult time to find room for a life beyond academe. "New faculty were frustrated by lack of opportunities to meet other new faculty" (Sorcinelli 1988, p. 128).

Lack of collegial support
Isolation and intellectual understimulation reflect a general lack of collegiality experienced by new faculty. A number of studies have shown that new faculty consistently complain about lack of collegial support (Boice 1991a, 1992; Fink 1984; Reynolds 1992; Sorcinelli 1988, 1992; Turner and Boice 1987). A new faculty member in a study conducted by Whitt (1991) provides some insight into the general lack of collegiality and the subsequent isolation new faculty face: "My picture of the culture here is one of fragmentation, probably due to the fact that everyone must do research, and research happens to be a very lonely type of thing unless people team together" (p. 183).

For some new faculty, lack of collegiality is experienced not so much through a lack of contact with colleagues as through negative interactions. Boice noted that, "Newcomers . . . routinely reported hostile comments from colleagues with more seniority" (1991a, p. 32). Relatedly, Boice pointed out the following complaints about senior faculty: (1) senior faculty routinely excluded new faculty from departmental decision making; (2) senior faculty complained about new faculty seeking professional visibility; (3) senior faculty were disinterested in the research of new faculty; (4) senior faculty complained of the narrow research interests of new faculty; and (5) senior faculty proclaimed that teaching and research were mutually incompatible.

Work loads and time constraints

New faculty consistently comment about lack of time to pursue scholarly work. As van der Bogert noted, "New faculty were frustrated by the lack of time. They could not do all the course preparation they felt was necessary; they greeted questions on how much time they were spending on scholarly work with laughs" (1991, p. 68). For the most part, new faculty tend to spend much more time on lecture preparation and teaching than expected (Boice 1991b; Turner and Boice 1987). Others reported high amounts of stress related to work loads in general (Sorcinelli 1988; Whitt 1991). Mager and Myers highlighted that 74 percent of new education professors reportedly spend more then 50 hours per week on work-related tasks, and 38 percent spend more than 60 hours per week (1983). New faculty may find it disheartening to learn that pressures from faculty work loads are unlikely to lessen any significant degree over one's academic career (Baldwin and Blackburn 1981).

Informal aspects of organizational culture

Not only do new faculty have to learn the formalized policies and practices of their institution, but additionally, "new professors have much to learn about the informal operations and modes of conduct in the complex organization known as a college or university" (Baldwin 1979, p. 19). As we noted in section one, an organization's culture is more than the formal rules, codes, and regulations that direct members' behaviors; culture is also those traditions, beliefs, and practices passed on from one generation to the next—typically learned through oral histories. "Much of what is expected of [faculty] is unstated and unwritten" (Whitt 1991, p. 179):

In a certain faculty lunchroom in a major university school of nursing there was a central table with five to seven chairs around it, and around the perimeter of the room were additional chairs. Senior faculty members usually brought their lunches and sat around the center table at noon. Junior faculty who chose to bring their lunches and eat in the lunchroom were never so bold as to sit at the center table without invitation; they sat around the perimeter of the room. The newcomers to the lunchroom were faced with several questions: What rites of passage existed for junior faculty to gain access to the central table? What were the rules that governed group behavior within the setting and how were these determined (Elay Group 1988, p. 88)?

As a novice, the new professor may find the organizational culture difficult to fully comprehend. "What is valued may be misunderstood or perhaps understood all too clearly" (Mager and Myers 1982, p. 104). The rites of passage and informal rules that govern group behavior are a significant concern in a number of areas. For example, what is the role of a new faculty member at departmental meetings, at faculty senate or union meetings, or at divisional meetings, or, simply, how is one expected to deal with departmental office assistants? These are the additional kinds of informal dilemmas posed to the new faculty member—most of which must be negotiated through trial and error.

Dimensional Analysis

One way of looking at the organizational socialization of new faculty is to analyze their experiences in light of Van Maanen and Schein's "dimensions of organizational socialization" discussed in section three. For example, the loneliness and intellectual understimulation frequently experienced by new faculty arguably are the by-products of the hyperindividualized nature of early organizational socialization. Individual socialization, as opposed to collective socialization, places new organizational members within a "sink or swim" setting in which they must "hit the ground running" to succeed (Whitt 1991). Individual socialization typically is associated with organizational hierarchies where the organizational participant must learn certain skills, attitudes, and values to handle complex tasks before moving on to a higher status. Passage to a higher status involves winning the approval of organizational gatekeepers who evaluate each participant on an individual basis.

The lack of collegial support reported by new faculty can be linked to the individualized nature of their socialization which, for many faculty, stands in sharp contrast to their graduate school experiences. "The rich stimulation of graduate study days is exchanged sometimes for intellectual bareness when the graduate student moves from a collection of desks in a shared room to a private office as an assistant professor" (Mager and Myers 1982, p. 105).

Complaints about faculty work loads and time constraints can be interpreted as an emphasis upon disjunctive versus serial socialization processes. Disjunctive processes are those where little to no mentoring is offered. Serial socialization depends more upon role models to assist the newcomer in learning the ropes. Evidence suggests that work loads are fairly stable over the span of faculty life (Baldwin and Blackburn 1981). Yet, in spite of demanding expectations, many faculty survive and indeed excel. Serial socialization can assist new faculty by utilizing the experience and expertise of senior faculty through a mentoring relationship. We discuss faculty mentoring in greater detail in section six.

The unspoken codes, norms, and mores which are essential for proper behavior as a new faculty member highlight the informal aspect of faculty organizational socialization. Informal socialization is typical of a laissez-faire experience where the norms are expected to be learned through trial and error. Formal socialization processes are less ambiguous and typically result in lesser degrees of stress. As is the case with faculty work loads, faculty mentors can play a positive role in helping new faculty learn the subtleties of everyday life and survive the early years of socialization. In this light, faculty mentors may be seen as trail guides who help recruits negotiate their way over the organizational mountain passes that are the early years of faculty life.

Summary
The recruitment and selection process serves as a rite of passage for faculty candidates as they seek organizational entry. The process is one of aligning values between organizational

TABLE 2

Summary of Dimensional Analysis

PROBLEM	DIMENSION OF SOCIALIZATION	TACTICAL SUGGESTION
1. Loneliness/ understimulation	Collective socialization	Utilize greater group involvement in new faculty socialization
2. Heavy work loads/ time constraints	Serial socialization	Improve faculty mentoring
3. Learning through trial and error	Formal socialization	Clearly articulate the organizational goals and messages

goals and objectives and candidates' skills, abilities, and interests. Once this process is complete, the outsider becomes the new recruit—the novice.

As new faculty enter the strange social milieu of academe, they face another set of rites of passage as they struggle to move from the role of initiate to full member. The first few years are marked by social and intellectual isolation as they try to prove themselves worthy of inclusionary rights. These first few years are the most stressful of all the career stages within the professorate. The socialization that occurs in these early years is not just a formalized process but also involves many complex social mores and norms that must be mastered. What is the role of new faculty at faculty meetings? Who sits where? What are the social customs of informal faculty gatherings? These are just a few of the less formalized social learning processes that new faculty encounter.

THE RITUAL PROCESS OF TENURE AND PROMOTION

*All of us are under ritual's sway; absolutely none of us
stands outside of ritual's symbolic jurisdiction. . . . Older
than written history, they [rituals] are what remains once
the stones and columns have disintegrated and the ruins
have been cleared* (McLaren 1986, pp. 34-35).

Socialization involves learning the various roles one must
enact in a multitude of complex social settings. With each role
comes scripts or clues about how to enact these roles. Rituals
are a major form of socialization. From a cultural perspective,
promotion and tenure is a ritual process that serves as a rite
of passage for new faculty.

Turner described such a process as "rituals of status ele-
vation" (1977). He pointed out how the initiate was "conveyed irreversibly from a lower to a higher position in an insti-
tutionalized system of such positions" (p. 167). The ritual
process is interactive. Organizational actors have opportunities
to shape rituals, and although a ritual such as tenure and promotion has existed in academe for generations, the process
also changes through time.

In the first part of this section we consider the ritual process
of the tenure and promotion years. A ritual is not simply an
event but involves preparation and planning on the part of
a number of social actors. Consequently, we consider the ritual process (a) for the initiate, (b) for the institution, and (c)
for the discipline.

In the second part of this section, we specifically consider
the ritual event—the year-long analysis and decision of an
initiate's dossier, credentials, and qualifications. Obviously,
we are aware that the ritual will differ from institution to institution. The process, for example, will be different for a community college professor and an initiate at a research university. Our goal is to lessen the mystification involved in tenure
and promotion with the intent of providing suggestions to
improve the process. Accordingly, we develop the following
scenario of the tenure years for assistant professor Barbara
Mara, a mythical professor at a large university.

The Tenure and Promotion Years
For the initiate
Although everyone enters the ritual process with the awareness that eventually a judgment will be made about whether
one receives tenure and promotion, most individuals are

---

aware dimly of what is required of them. Barbara Mara, for example, initially was pleased to have attained employment at her institution; indeed, given the tight job market she was glad to have found a position in a respected department. She did not have many impressions of the university. Her interview had been a nervous blur of meetings with senior faculty and the dean. After the phone call from the dean offering her the position, she had not heard from anyone and did not want to be a bother, so she didn't call anyone either. But she had so many questions! She assumed once she arrived on campus she would receive an orientation where she might find some answers.

Professor Mara found out indirectly what was expected of her. The departmental secretary had been a big help. The department chair had said his door was always open, but he always seemed so busy; she talked with him little more than she talked with any of the other senior faculty. Mara knew, of course, that she had to teach three courses a semester, and that one of these was a graduate seminar. Everyone said research was "important," although Mara wasn't sure what to expect. She remembered asking a senior professor about how many articles she should try to publish for tenure, and he had responded that they were not "bean counters. It's quality that counts." She was not sure at all what "service" meant.

Mara was placed on two collegewide committees. When she attended the meetings, faculty arrived late and left early. Undergraduates constantly seemed to be waiting outside her door for an appointment. She liked teaching, but she was surprised at how much time it took. A handful of graduate students were always waiting for feedback on a proposal, dissertation chapter, or job reference. Mara never seemed to have time for reflection about research—much less for a personal life.

No one talked to Mara about her teaching, but senior faculty continually seemed to remind her how important research was to get tenure. There was one other untenured professor in the department, but his interests were different; she wasn't sure why, but sometimes she felt that she was competing with him.

Mara had sent an article to a journal that was based on her dissertation but she heard nothing for six months. She patiently waited to hear about the status of the piece, and after another month or two she received a short letter stating that the article was rejected because "the methodology was weak and the findings insubstantial." She reworked the article and sent it to another journal and waited an additional six months. When she heard nothing after another month, she called the editor. The editor's secretary informed Mara that they were delinquent in their work and were swamped with submissions, but that some decision probably would be made within six months.

In the meantime, Mara had submitted two proposals for presentations at a conference. Both presentations were accepted, but she did not receive funding to go to the conference because all the college's funds had been spent. The department chair told Barbara that the procedure was to request funds at the start of the school year and that the next year, perhaps, there would be funds available for the conference.

After spending personal funds to attend the conference, Mara had three people in the audience for her first paper presentation. Although she had spent an inordinate amount of time on the papers, one of the three in the audience fell asleep during the presentation. The second paper received a better audience, but the discussant for the panel went over time on his interpretation of another speaker's idea and never mentioned Mara's paper. One person approached Mara at the end of the session and asked for a copy of her paper. She had heard that she should bring handouts of the presentation since it was a good way to network and have one's work read, so she rushed to give the person one of the 50 copies she had carried from home.

A senior faculty member had told Mara that the dean wanted everyone to attend the university's reception at the conference. "He practically takes attendance," the senior professor had laughed. The room was packed with people when Mara entered. The only individuals who looked familiar were departmental colleagues, but they seemed to ignore her. She stood alone in a corner of the room and wondered, "Is this really worth it? Is this really how I want to spend my life?"

For the institution

Barbara Mara's experience may not be an exact replica of a specific individual, but there are too many elements that ring true to ignore the vignette. Indeed, the preceding sections have discussed problems of loneliness, lack of support, weak

Professor Mara found out indirectly what was expected of her. The departmental secretary had been a big help.

mentoring, and other problems that we have portrayed here. The vignette underscores dysfunctional socialization in that the novice indirectly has learned a lot about the nature of her institution and of academe in general. But are these the lessons that should be taught? We retrace Mara's steps with an eye toward improvement.

Any new hire will have many questions, all of which cannot be answered prior to one's arrival on campus. However, varying forms of written and verbal information can be helpful. A handbook that outlines basic services provides an initial orientation. "Survival guides" and books discuss the experiences of new faculty (Boice 1992; Jarvis 1991; Schuster and Wheeler 1990). Such information can be extremely helpful in aiding an individual to come to grips with the often-oblique system of needs and demands of academe.

Another form of information revolves around the department chair or senior faculty member. A delicate balance lies between paternalism and the hands-off attitude exhibited by Mara's department chair. We will return to this point in section eight, but someone in a senior position should be involved actively in looking out for a junior person's welfare. At a minimum, a few phone calls prior to the person's arrival to see how a transition might be smoothed seems prudent.

Upon arrival, formal and informal feedback mechanisms must be in place. The guessing game that tenure and promotion has become in many institutions is unnecessary at a minimum and, at worst, unproductive for the candidate and the institution. To be sure, the number of articles that one needs to publish is not akin to "counting beans," but the institution should be able to provide systematic, verifiable advice to *all* tenure-track faculty.

One individual hears, for example, that the publication of one's dissertation does not count toward tenure; another individual is told that the publication of a book—even one's dissertation—ensures promotion and tenure. One professor says only refereed articles count toward tenure, and another states that two non-refereed articles are equal to one refereed article. One person states that co-authored articles are worthless, and another person says that it is important to co-author an article with a graduate student as a sign of mentoring.

On a grander scale, the institution may say that teaching is paramount, but a tenure-track candidate has a friend who is denied tenure because he has not published enough. No one says that service is important, for example, but the junior faculty member serves on more committees than anyone else in the department. Would a system that cares for individuals create work that jeopardizes someone's eventual success?

The point here is not that anyone is trying purposefully to deceive the candidate, or that a dean, a department chair, or senior faculty member are shirking responsibilities. Rather, the tenure system is an odd potpourri of folk wisdom and half truths that far too often provoke bewilderment in a candidate trying to balance a multitude of duties. Ultimately, promotion and tenure depends on human judgment, and what often irks senior faculty is the idea that simple numbers—"it takes two articles per year"—will determine if someone succeeds. At the same time, candidates should be able to receive verifiable advice, such as, "Only one person has ever gotten tenure with less than four refereed articles, and that person won a Nobel Prize."

Our purpose in this text is not to determine institutional priorities toward promotion and tenure, but to point out that those priorities should be clear. If one's dissertation does not count toward tenure, then all candidates and all individuals on promotion and tenure committees should know such information. If the publication of a textbook or a manual does not help toward tenure, then again, everyone involved in the promotion and tenure process should have such information. Obviously, discrepancies may exist across colleges. A handbook may be slighted in the social sciences and be important in agriculture. Our simple point is that the system should provide systematic, informed commentary to all candidates and individuals involved in the promotion and tenure process.

Information, advice, and suggestions should be conveyed in two forms. Informal conversations with individuals lessen the hierarchical nature of senior-junior faculty relationships and provide the sense of an ongoing dialogue about an individual's progress. Too often a candidate arrives at a third- or fourth-year review and no one was aware that he or she did not publish because of service and teaching commitments.

At the same time, a formal discussion should be held once a year. In a system ostensibly based on collegiality, formal evaluation often seems anathema to junior and senior faculty alike. However, in the absence of such a meeting, the consequence is the guessing game in which Barbara Mara became involved. A formal meeting once a year enables a department chair to plan for the future and consider relief for teaching for an individual, and allows the candidate to air any problems he or she has.

Depending on the size of one's faculty, it may be difficult for a dean to schedule individual meetings with faculty. At the same time, one wonders what can be more important than a decision that potentially involves millions of institutional dollars (assuming the candidate receives tenure and stays at the institution). We are suggesting that the care and nurturing of junior faculty receives the highest priority by a college dean. In doing so, the dean is able to develop a specific climate within the college that fosters collegiality and concern for the community.

An orientation for all new faculty is one way to offer initial information about the college and facilitate networking. An orientation also might be developed in an ongoing format, because often the information provided during one's first encounters on campus only take hold once one is involved in the process. For example, it is helpful at the first meeting to highlight the fact that there is a teaching center on campus to which a novice might turn; this information will be even more worthwhile after a semester or two when the initiate begins to recognize his or her teaching weaknesses. The main point is that although a college dean should not try to fill the function of a departmental chair or senior mentor, the dean should be in close touch with each tenure-track candidate to provide counsel and advice when necessary.

For the discipline

We turn to a discussion of the culture of the discipline because it plays a crucial role in the success or failure of a candidate's promotion and tenure. The disciplinary—even more than the institutional—culture is where meetings, journals, book publishing, and scholarly networking occur. Again, Barbara Mara's vignette may not be true for people in every aspect, but there is some truth in all of the examples, and we can learn more than simply suggesting that it is impolite to fall asleep when a colleague is speaking.

As with the discussion about the institution, our purpose is not to suggest standards for journal publication. However, all writers, and especially younger scholars, need clear feedback about the problems encountered in a journal submission. To simply say that the "methodology was weak" does not help the author, and a disciplinary culture that creates affirming socialization experiences will try to enlighten rather than condemn. Further, the abnormal delay in judging articles that often happens in scholarly journals is again, not merely impolite, but seriously jeopardizes a candidate's chances for tenure. If a journal is "swamped with submissions" and will take a year to review someone's article, it is incumbent upon the editor to let the author know immediately so that he or she may pursue other options.

Senior scholars from the institution and the discipline have a scholarly obligation to advise junior colleagues about publication. As we all know, publication does not merely depend upon the worth of one's ideas. Networking is important and an understanding of which journal is appropriate for a specific kind of article is essential. There is little point to maintain an academic guessing game for junior scholars as they submit one article after another to journals that are ill-suited for their research and professional advancement.

Conferences are one of the more stressful professional activities that a young scholar encounters. As Barbara Mara observed, many people believed conferences were important for "networking," but Mara was unsure just how to go about the task. One way is for session discussants to provide more systematic feedback to a young scholar's paper than merely a cursory glance. Another possibility is for the disciplinary organization to create informal alliances between senior scholars and newcomers if for no other reason than to create a friendly face in a sea of anonymity. A meeting for newcomers and sessions on publishing held by editors of major journals are examples of positive actions that a professional association may develop.

As with every suggestion, "networking" should not have to be a magical process that a candidate discovers on his or her own. Indeed, as we shall see, networking is essential for most individuals if they are to be successfully socialized and granted promotion and tenure.

The Ritual Year
For the initiate
During the summer before her sixth year, Barbara Mara began to assemble her files. She had heard that they needed to be submitted "sometime in the fall," and with the rush of activities to which she had become accustomed at the start of fall

semester, she was sure she would not have time to do an adequate job on the files if she waited.

She was surprised about how much information was needed. She had to submit all course evaluations, a list of every committee she had served on, and all her publications and presentations. She had her publications and presentations on her vita, so that was no problem. However, she barely could remember all the committee work she had performed; she only listed some major committees since she had learned that service was not so important.

She was disappointed that she did not have more written information about her teaching, but she had not known it was necessary. She had become a good teacher, and twice during the last two years she even had received a round of applause at the end of the term from her large lecture class. Those moments were the highlights of her career at the university, but she had nothing to show for it. She regretted that she had not received any written commentary from students, but she figured that her teaching scores would suffice.

Mara worried a lot about her references. She had been told that she needed to list six people in her field who were qualified to judge her work. It was funny and depressing that after six years she still had to struggle about whom to suggest. Two professors knew her work quite well and a third was her dissertation advisor, but she barely knew the other three individuals she had listed.

At the start of the fall semester her chair had said that he was sure the file would "fly right through," since most of her previous evaluations had been fair. He promised her he would take a look at her files when he got a chance. The new dean worried Barbara, but the school year started and the pace of her life picked up.

The Friday before the college committee's Monday meeting the department chair hurried into Mara's office to tell her that the college had a new format and she needed to change the way she had presented her files. He also said that the dean's office had been late in requesting letters of reference and she still did not have two letters in her file. She spent the weekend reworking her files and worrying that the other letters would arrive.

She received a letter from the dean a month later stating that her candidacy had been denied. Although her teaching and service were "adequate," her research was viewed as marginal by "scholars in the field." Mara felt alternately angry and sad and wondered what now awaited her.

For the institution

Professor Mara's initiation ritual ended in failure. The previous segment outlined what kind of activities might have been helpful. But there also are points of intervention and support that might be offered once the ritual year has begun. For example, the forms the institution requires a candidate to fill out should be clear well before the actual date the forms are needed. The department chair or senior scholar should review the documents to ensure that the necessary information is presented as clearly and logically as possible. The candidate needs to know in his or her first year that all work-related information must be kept so that when the forms are filled in, all of one's committee work, for example, will be listed.

The dean's office needs to manage the process so that last-minute changes or gaps do not occur. A faculty member who is on a year's leave of absence may be unable to fill out a letter of review, but such an absence in a candidate's file reflects poorly on the candidate. A fascimile or express letter to an outside reviewer asking for an immediate evaluation of a candidate reflects poorly on the college as well as the candidate.

A new dean certainly has the prerogative to advocate for the change of promotion and tenure standards, but these changes need to be conducted fairly, clearly, and with full discussion with those individuals under review. In Mara's case, what was unfortunate was that she did not have better documentation of her service and teaching, that perhaps her letters were not as strong as they could have been, and that she had been led to believe from previous reviews that her work met the standards of the institution. If nothing had changed in her work habits from her previous review to the time for a tenure decision, it seems questionable that she should be denied tenure. Finally, the manner in which the dean communicated to Mara probably could have been improved. Surely a formal letter is necessary, but as with the symbols present during initial interviews, the manner in which one treats the initiate after a tenure decision is a potent symbol of how the institution values individuals. A meeting with the individual as well as job counseling and support throughout the final year seem warranted.

For the discipline

One point remains on which to be commented, and it relates to the culture of the discipline: scholarly advancement and review. Disciplines have a multitude of ways in which the members interact. It would be naive—not to say mistaken—to assume that the only way one becomes known in a field is through one's research activities. A host of informal and formal mechanisms exist that facilitate individuals getting acquainted. Reviewing articles and presentations, committee work, chairing sessions, and social activities are examples of disciplinary experiences that socialize the initiate to the culture of academic work. These are also activities that enable younger scholars to come into contact with senior colleagues. It is incumbent on the discipline to incorporate new members as a means of professional advancement so that at the time of tenure review, the individual is known in the field.

The fact remains, however, that a scholar reviews a candidate's credentials essentially based on the worth of one's published material. It seems absurd to send outside reviewers everything (or nothing) an individual has written and ask for their commentary in a week's time; such a task is especially difficult if the reviewer has no acquaintance with the candidate. During the tenure years the candidate should be encouraged to offer—and again, senior scholars should welcome—occasional review of an individual's work. Such a relationship informs the senior scholar about the junior colleague's work and provides ongoing analysis so that the novice may improve. At the time of tenure review, then, the candidate will avoid the problem faced by Barbara Mara and will have a handful of senior colleagues who can comment confidently on the individual's skills and abilities.

Summary

We reiterate that this section is not intended to dilute standards or reform institutional beliefs about tenure. However, the ritual process of tenure and promotion is embedded in a cultural system that can be improved dramatically. The mystification and misinformation that candidates encounter on the way to tenure review is unnecessary and benefits no one.

The systematic analysis and review of the tenure process should be a standard task of the provost's office and the faculty senate. Disciplinary associations also need to develop thoughtful critiques of ways in which they might specifically aid their junior members. Rituals of transition in traditional societies ensure success: An initiate passes from adolescence to adulthood. Promotion and tenure cannot be a similar ritual because even with the best of efforts, an institution may decide that an individual is not well-suited for permanent employment. But as the preceding sections have shown, we surely can perform better than we have. In section eight we return to this theme, but we now turn to the system of socialization after tenure.

POST-TENURE SOCIALIZATION: SENIOR FACULTY AS LEARNERS

Socialization takes place from the womb to tomb. It is a recurrent and lifelong process taking many forms and occurring across a wide range of settings. Exiting one setting moves one into another, and socialization begins anew (Van Maanen 1983, p. 213).

When a faculty member receives tenure, organizational life changes. The same may be said about moving from associate professor to full professor. For a full professor the organizational culture is seen from a different perspective, from a position ostensibly higher up on the organizational hierarchy. Associate and full professors have the ability to assume a variety of roles—mentor, trusted colleague, department chair, institutional leader, and disciplinary scholar. Based on their extensive knowledge of the organizational culture and history, they are in a powerful position to shape the realities of others.

And yet, as a never-ending process, even the most experienced organizational members undergo socializing experiences that require growth and change. Culture is dynamic, and organizational learning needs to be ongoing for all members. In this section we examine the post-tenure faculty member along two lines: as a socializer of other faculty and as an organizational member involved in ongoing socialization.

Even the most experienced organizational members undergo socializing experiences that require growth and change.

Senior Faculty as Socializers

We referred in the previous section to the roles senior faculty might play in the advancement of their junior colleagues. If the preceding section was more instrumental, focusing on specific actions individuals might take, this section is more strategic. We consider the manner in which an institution and its senior colleagues might approach the task of mentoring. Specifically, we argue that senior faculty not only have advice and wisdom to impart but also need to be intellectual learners who value the input and ideas of their junior colleagues. We examine three roles senior faculty fill in their capacity as culture bearers: the symbolic leader, the trail guide, and the oral historian. We highlight how socialization may be viewed in a bidirectional manner so that individuals are not simply homogenized to cultural norms but valued as important new members to the community.

The symbolic leader

"It is a truism in American higher education that its managers—department chairpersons, deans, or academic vice presidents—almost always come from faculty ranks" (Tucker and Bryan 1988, p. 81). From these positions they are able to shape the realities of others by offering their own vision of the institution. Because of their experience and knowledge of the organizational culture, senior faculty are capable of giving symbolic meaning to events that the faculty novice might see as perplexing or chaotic. They do so by focusing attention on aspects of the institutional culture that are familiar and meaningful to the college community (Bensimon, Neumann, and Birnbaum 1989).

Leadership not only is a symbolic word. Senior faculty have the ability to set standards by enacting those standards themselves. A faculty member who holds an endowed chair, for example, provides a potent symbol when she regularly teaches a first-year seminar. A full professor who seeks out a junior colleague for honest advice about an article on which he is working highlights the importance of conversation across levels. A department chair who solicits input from junior colleagues about the nature of the curriculum or what courses should be offered in the summer has the potential to impress on the novice that everyone's ideas are important and can effect change in the institution.

The converse, of course, also is painfully true. A novice all too often is socialized to a norm where senior faculty have light teaching loads and junior faculty are supposed to silently receive criticism from their elders and have no voice in departmental or college affairs. To lead by symbol in the manner we suggest offers the initiate a fundamental opportunity to shape the culture.

The trail guide
Senior faculty find themselves in a position where other less-experienced faculty seek their advice and knowledge about the cultural mores of the organization. In this regard, senior faculty may find themselves in the role of mentor or trusted colleague. We have considered in section five how individuals might respond as a mentor with regard to publication, teaching, and other matters.

As a trusted and respected colleague, senior faculty also may deal with cultural issues that pertain to the organization and the individual. How often do I have to go to the office? How should I dress for the office or class? What is my role at faculty meetings? Do I have to go to faculty socials? How do I juggle all these tasks? These are just a few of the questions that might be posed to mentors.

Such questions often seem trivial, but they form the core of the implicit cultural web that binds members. The individual who shows up at her office once a week when the norm is that everyone makes a daily appearance or the fellow who wears shorts and sneakers when others work in ties and slacks create problems for themselves that they may not realize. If an individual wants to violate a norm, that is surely their decision. However, they at least should be aware they are doing so; often, cultural transgressions are not purposeful. Most individuals only have a passive awareness of an organization's culture, and they only discover the strength of culture when they have transgressed its bounds.

The informal conversations that take place at lunch, on the road, or at the faculty mailboxes also are implicit indicators to an individual about the culture of the organization. Senior faculty have the ability to create an inclusive culture where newcomer interests get voiced, heard, and honored. As we will consider in the next section, such a point is especially important with regard to underrepresented groups.

Mentoring, then, is more involved than merely acting as a trusted colleague and dispensing advice; the mentoring relationship implies commitment and a desire to learn from the novice as well. "It consists of regular meetings and of useful advice and advocacy between pairs of colleagues over periods of at least a year" (Boice 1993, p. 306). Whether or not colleges adopt a formal mentor program, senior colleagues are a tremendous source of cultural and professional guidance for the novice, and we are suggesting that this role be developed in a more systematic way than typically occurs.

The oral historian

Much of what faculty need to know about life in their institutions will not appear in the faculty handbook, the mission statement, or the various guides to institutional policies and procedures. Even if institutions adopt the procedures suggested in this text, an academic institution still maintains an oral tradition. This knowledge is contained in the manifold stories or myths that pass from one faculty generation to the next. These organizational myths reveal much about the cultural fabric of the institution and can be a rich source of cultural knowledge. As Pettigrew notes:

Just as ritual may provide a shared experience of belonging and express and reinforce what is valued, so myth also plays its crucial role in the continuous processes of establishing and maintaining what is legitimate and that which is labelled unacceptable in an organizational culture (1983, p. 96).

In popular usage, myth implies falsehood. In the sense of myth applied here—the anthropological notion—myth is a narrative of events which often have a sacred quality. Myths link the present to the past.

Based on their time in academe and experiences at their specific institution, senior faculty hold a wealth of institutional myths. Brown noted in her study of organizational socialization and storytelling that as members move through the socialization process, the stories they tell tend to relate more closely to organizational values and culture. "These stories served to integrate the activities of the organization by presenting specific or generalized events as a part of organizational life" (1985, p. 38). This knowledge is passed on to faculty typically in informal settings where storytelling seems best suited.

As with any story, it is open to interpretation and change. Indeed, faculty ought to utilize their roles as oral historians not to pass on simplemindedly treasured myths of the past, but that these myths be used to examine and change the present. Rather than a story that is to be passively accepted, such stories have the capability to be points for analysis and change. The glorification of the "good old days" may not appear that way to those of us who were excluded from those days; at the same time, an institution bereft of history is an institution without clear markers about identity and ideology. The analysis of the past enables junior and senior colleagues to embark on plans for the future.

The Ongoing Socialization of Senior Faculty

- A full professor receives a memo from the president saying that from now on the administration will only use electronic mail in interoffice correspondence to save time and money. Although the professor heard about electronic mail a few years ago, he has never bothered to hook up and consequently feels a bit adrift by the president's note.

- In the dean's address at the start of the school year, she pointed out the financial straits the college was in and said she expected all faculty to bring in grants. A full professor has never written a proposal in his life and has no idea where to begin.

- A young professor in the department asked an older colleague to read a draft of an article, but the article had so many new ideas he did not know how to critique it. His mood alternated between sadness that he was behind the times and anger at the younger professor's enamor of trendy ideas.

At least three possible organizational responses exist with regard to these examples. One possibility is for the organization to do nothing. A second response is to recognize a problem and hold a workshop or two for senior professors. The third reaction is to treat these issues as cultural dilemmas that pertain to socialization.

Clearly, the first response is inadequate. The second response is functional in nature and responds to an immediate problem: Someone does not know how to use the computer, so the institution develops a training class to bring individuals up to speed. Although such classes are helpful and necessary, they are reactive in nature and do not adequately treat the underlying cultural issues.

The problems presented here are common dilemmas that confront all senior faculty in all types of organizations. If an institution is able to develop a culture where socialization is seen as ongoing and where all individuals are learners as well as teachers, then the institution will develop proactive strategies for dealing with socialization in the same way that they have developed strategies for aiding younger faculty.

The benefits of such an approach are that the "problem" is not seen as residing in the individual—the senior professor is "behind the times." Rather than using stopgap and reactive measures, the institution is able to plan for the future. As we shall discuss, younger faculty also are able to be seen in a different light; they often will have skills, theories, and methodologies they will be able to teach senior faculty so the hierarchical nature of senior/junior relationships will be changed. And the institution will benefit from a culture where individuals embrace change rather than one where changes are fought because senior faculty seek to maintain the status quo.

We are not painting an organizational utopia. We noted that even the best socialization for younger faculty will result in some individual departures. Similarly, not all senior faculty will buy into the concept of themselves as learners who need to be involved in ongoing socialization. Obviously, changes in any number of areas are difficult for institutional members, and it is especially hard for those people who have worked for a great number of years. The life cycles of individuals also interact with any organizational culture. No matter how strategic an organization, some individuals will resist change because of personal circumstances. However, far too often an organization responds to dilemmas such as those outlined above either by developing a temporary response or by not reacting at all. What we are proposing is a philosophy of how an institution might build a community of concern where difference is honored and the culture exists in a structure oriented for change and renewal. We return to this topic in section eight, but we offer four areas where culture and socialization are especially important for senior faculty.

Mentoring. It has become common to point out that faculty are trained in a discipline but they are rarely trained to advise and counsel undergraduate students (Bess 1978; Schuster 1990b). The same point holds true for the mentoring of junior faculty. As with any activity, some individuals will be more adept as mentors than others. However, everyone should have basic knowledge and advice about how to help junior faculty.

A yearly workshop is one way to offer information to faculty about how to work with tenure-track faculty. Such a workshop is also a good time to highlight what is and is not needed with regard to tenure. Training sessions for department chairs also are helpful and allow individuals to speak amongst themselves about what they do to aid junior faculty. In larger departments it is incumbent for senior faculty to get together to decide who will work specifically with a younger person and the kinds of activities that might be developed to aid the individual.

Our point here is that an institution cannot ask of its senior faculty what they are not prepared to do. Workshops that highlight the changing face of academe with regard to women and people of color are greatly important. Individuals are unique, and just as faculty need to understand how to reach different groups of students they also need training with regard to how to work with newer members of the faculty. These types of workshops emphasize the philosophy of bidirectionality where an institution seeks to enable older faculty to understand the needs of people who might be quite different from themselves rather than assume that all groups are the same and have the same needs. Such activities also are potent organizational symbols about what the institution values.

Academic leadership. Carlyle may have thought that some "men" are born leaders and others followers, but he was not speaking of academic leadership (1841). There are various forms of leadership that an individual may fulfill in academe. To enable all individuals to fill these roles some form of training is necessary. If we assume that an individual needs specific help achieving tenure, then it seems logical that there also will be activities that will aid the post-tenure faculty in professional advancement.

The kind of activities that might be beneficial are training sessions for faculty governance, an overview of the manifold problems that confront academe, and many of the latest changes that are being implemented in colleges and universities. Unless one's area of interest happens to be higher education, faculty do not have much of an understanding of the diversity in higher education and the array of governance arrangements that exist. To the extent that senior faculty can develop a comparative perspective about the nature of their institutions, they will be better able to understand differences and create change.

Interchange. Sabbaticals and leaves of absence remain the preferred way for renewal and training of senior faculty (Clark 1983). We reaffirm this point. In economic hard times institutions have begun to look at sabbaticals as one area that might be cut to save income. The fact remains that to keep individuals current in their field or to develop new areas of inquiry, individuals need time away from teaching and the multitude of duties that encompass faculty life. To remove sabbaticals as an option will only retard faculty learning in skills needed for the future.

However, to reaffirm the need of sabbaticals does not imply that sabbatical policies must be left unquestioned. The idea that an individual automatically receives a sabbatical or that any topic is worthy of a paid leave of absence seems as absurd as doing away with the policy. Obviously, who decides what is worthy of investigation is a sensitive issue. We raise the point that sabbaticals, faculty interchanges, and leaves of absence should not be considered perfunctory rewards, but key components of resocialization.

New pedagogic and curricular forms. Here again is an area in which younger faculty might offer a roundtable or talk on current thinking in a specific area. Teachers also might become involved in a forum about how to improve teaching methods. In many respects, both of these areas are examples of instances where junior and senior colleagues may work together as colleagues rather than as advisee-mentor. A faculty member who has taught for 20 years may find a workshop on teaching and learning as helpful as does the junior faculty member.

To the extent possible, departments also might regularly schedule interchange and observation in one another's classes. Some institutions have developed a system where senior faculty sit in on a class of a tenure-track faculty member to pass judgment about the worth of one's teaching. This is the kind of unidirectional socialization experience that we would like to weaken. The implicit lesson of such an experience is that senior faculty are judges, and that junior faculty have nothing of worth that they might say to senior faculty about teaching. Instead, a system where every faculty member sits in another's class offers the possibility of honest interchange across ranks.

Summary

We have offered strategies for post-tenure socialization that hinge on the idea of teachers as learners. We recognize the pitfalls of some of the ideas we have proposed. Some senior faculty will resent, if not refuse, to have junior faculty sit in their classes. A junior faculty member who presents a paper on a new area of inquiry may be attacked by a senior professor who rejects his or her ideas. To suggest that sabbatical policies be reconsidered may allow the intrusion of administrators in an area that faculty see as their own.

However, we are suggesting strategic responses for tenured faculty so that institutions might be able to develop specific policies that are unique to their own college or university. As with the previous section, we are not advocating a specific institutional policy, but rather we have offered a strategic response. Post-tenure socialization occurs whether or not the institution decides to do it. We have suggested that institutions build a conscious framework for socialization that is shaped by and helps shape the organization's culture.

THE SOCIALIZATION OF WOMEN FACULTY
AND FACULTY OF COLOR

It is curious and worth at least a moment's consideration, that even schools with no women on their faculties are symbolized as cherishing mothers. Even where there are women on the faculties, not they but a mystical female—Alma Mater—nourishes and disciplines her charges:

When we stood at boyhood's gate,
Shapeless in the hands of fate,
Thou dids't mold us, Dear Old State,
Into men!
Into men!

(Bernard 1964, p. 1)

Borders are set up to define the places that are safe and unsafe, to distinguish us from them. A border is a dividing line, a narrow strip along a steep edge. A borderland is a vague and undetermined place created by the emotional residue of an unnatural boundary. It is in a constant state of transition. The prohibited and forbidden are its inhabitants (Anzaldua 1987, p. 3).

We face at least two risks in this section. First, as two white men delineating the experiences of women and people of color, we run the risk of perpetuating cultural borders based on race and gender—creating an us/them dichotomy. Yet at the same time, we cannot deny that many women faculty—certainly not all—and many faculty of color—again, not all—face differing and unique challenges in negotiating their way through the academic world. As Anzaldua highlights in the preceding passage, differences such as race and gender are the residue of unnatural boundaries (1987). Few social organizations promote and sustain social boundaries as well as academe.

Second, because we are writing about "women" and "people of color," we run the risk of grouping everyone together, as if everyone who is different is similar. That is, one assumption might be that the challenges faced by women faculty are the same as those encountered by African-American or Native American faculty, or that Asian American faculty are similar to Latino/Latina faculty. We do not intend to homogenize difference. Often, the problems that women faculty encounter, for example, are unique to their experience. Indeed, as we shall discuss, recent research highlights that the challenges

Few social organizations promote and sustain social boundaries as well as academe.

that women of color face are unique to their own experience (James and Farmer 1993; Etter-Lewis 1993) and differ from that of male faculty of color and women faculty.

However, what all underrepresented groups face is an over-riding organizational culture that often is formed on historical and social patterns that are both white and male. Our goal in this section, then, is to highlight some of the socialization experiences of women faculty and faculty of color that tend to perpetuate social boundaries. We also discuss the rationale for an emphasis on socialization that honors difference.

The Revolving Door

Women and people of color clearly are underrepresented among the American professorate. This especially is true when tenured faculty positions are examined. Studies have shown that a higher proportion of tenure-track women faculty and faculty of color leave the tenure track prior to a tenure decision than do their white, male colleagues (Tack and Patitu 1992). While efforts have been made to recruit faculty from diverse groups, little has been done to examine the socialization experiences of women faculty and faculty of color.

Research has shown that women are more likely to be denied tenure or to leave academe altogether and, in general, exhibit differential progress (American Association of University Women 1989; Dwyer, Flynn, and Inman 1991; Rothblum 1988). The same can be said of people of color (Collins 1990; Jackson 1991; Suinn and Witt 1982). The tendency by women faculty and faculty of color to leave academe frequently is discussed in terms of a "revolving door": New faculty are hired, stay for a few years, become discouraged and leave, or are denied tenure and then leave (Cross 1991). The revolving door represents a socialization process that largely has failed for the organization and the novice. The result has been alienation and departure. What are the causes? What are the solutions?

Sources of Socialization Problems

Jensen noted that characteristics unique to women make their socialization into academic culture problematic because the professorate is overwhelmingly male (1982). Like Reynolds (1992), Jensen argued that women experience more of an acculturation process than a socialization process since they must alter much of their individual identity. As Aisenberg and

Harrington highlighted, women are, in many ways, "outsiders in the sacred grove" of academe (1988).

People of color frequently represent diverse cultural backgrounds and also face more of an acculturation process or, in the terminology employed here, transformative socialization (Luz Reyes and Halcon 1991; Tierney 1992c). With these larger concerns in mind, based on a review of the literature we have identified the following dilemmas related to the socialization of women and people of color: inadequate anticipatory socialization, weak mentoring relationships, fewer networking opportunities, divergent priorities, and additional work demands.

Inadequate anticipatory socialization

Some of the problems women and people of color face as faculty relate to anticipatory socialization (Turner and Thompson 1993). While we have primarily discussed the anticipatory phase in terms of graduate school, the undergraduate years also serve to introduce individuals to the prospective roles and expectations of various professions. For example, women faculty and faculty of color report that they were less often encouraged as undergraduates to pursue graduate work (Olsen 1991). Blackwell noted that one-third of all doctoral students receive assistantships, but only one-fifth of minority doctoral students receive such positions (1984).

A professor as a mentor is critically important in graduate school. Yet, underrepresented groups often have difficulty creating and sustaining such a relationship. Gender may pose dilemmas in developing helpful mentoring relationships (Aisenberg and Harrington 1988). Rose reported that women tend to have weaker ties with their academic mentors (1985). Clark and Corcoran noted a tendency for advisors and others to doubt a woman's potential for scholarly productivity (1986).

Weak mentoring as faculty

While women and people of color not only may face difficulties in developing mentoring relationships during undergraduate and graduate school years, the same also may be said of their experiences as new faculty. In a study conducted at the University of Wisconsin-Madison, lack of institutional support for faculty was reported as a major factor in attrition (Rausch et al. 1989). An ingredient in the support system

is, of course, mentoring relationships. Here again, lower percentages of faculty who left the institution reported receiving professional support from an informal mentor.

Melillo developed a profile of the typical academic woman based on subgroups selected from academic physicians and counseling psychologists and noted a general lack of suitable role models (1981). Simeone observed that women are more likely than men to be denied opportunities to be mentored by senior faculty (1987).

Few black academicians benefit from a protege-mentor relationship (Frierson 1990). Only one in eight black faculty members identify themselves with a mentor (Blackwell 1983, 1984). Washington and Harvey argued that the lack of effective sponsorship was a significant problem for African-American and Hispanic faculty (1989). "The usual protective network of sympathetic senior faculty often does not exist" (p. 26).

Fewer networking opportunities

In a study of 47 women and 43 men in tenure-track assistant professor positions in psychology at 60 universities, Rose reported that women consistently rated their networks as less effective in helping them to build a professional reputation (1985). Rose also noted that women had fewer ties to their previous institutions and had more women colleagues. One study reported that 47 percent of the black faculty surveyed revealed feelings of isolation and alienation (Anderson, Frierson, and Lewis 1979). "They do not feel particularly close to white colleagues and often obtain little professional or emotional support" (p. 100). The lack of professional support networks is, in part, a by-product of minority faculty being located at the periphery of teaching and research. "They are often in non-tenured positions or special programs for minorities" (Epps 1989, p. 25).

Divergent priorities

Some researchers have raised questions about whether women are socialized to recognize what activities are most important for academic success (Widom and Burke 1978). Men and women frequently have different expectations about how they allocate family and work time (Reynolds 1992). Boice found that women value teaching to a greater degree than men (forthcoming). In a study of university faculty,

Olsen discovered that minority faculty are more involved in service, white women are more involved in teaching, and white men are more involved in research (1991). Of course, one needs to remember that research tends to be rewarded; consequently, such work habits partially explain the differential rates of tenure and promotion as well as higher attrition for women and people of color.

Additional demands

Additional demands for women frequently revolve around family (McElrath 1992). For those women faculty who opt to have children, their academic careers become even more complicated. This is more true for women than it is for men, since it still is common practice in our society for women to handle the majority of child care responsibilities (Muller 1990). Often the academic world views academic work and child raising as incompatible. Frequently, this incompatibility forces women to decide between family or career (Rothblum 1988).

> . . . having both a family and an academic career is no simple matter. The tenure system in the United States was set up for male faculty, whose wives provided all the homemaking so that their husbands could devote their energies solely to academic career advancement (Bronstein, Rothblum, and Solomon 1993, p. 25).

For faculty of color, additional demands relate to serving on campus committees where they frequently are selected to increase representation (Banks 1984; Blackwell 1988; Gilbert 1990). For example, Aguirre surveyed 149 Chicano faculty in the southwest, reporting that 43 percent were involved in affirmative action or Mexican-American community-related committees and 57 percent were on committees related to the recruitment and retention of Chicano students (1987). Cross highlighted some of the problems Native American faculty experience because of expectations placed on them to serve as counselors and advocates for Indian students as well as representing Native American perspectives on various campus committees (1991).

Minority scholars face the difficult decision to be either strict academics, scholar-advocates, advocate-scholars, or strict advocates. On one hand, their decisions are shaped by an academic culture that expects objective detachment. And on the other hand, their communities need leaders who seek social action and political change (Garza 1987-1988).

Dimensional Analysis

How can Van Mannen and Schein's dimensions of organizational socialization discussed in section three be utilized in understanding the problems faced by women faculty and faculty of color? One problem identified is inadequate anticipatory socialization. All six of the dimensions may be helpful here, but in particular, an emphasis upon serial socialization processes seems appropriate. Serial socialization relates to providing role models who help to initiate newcomers to the organization. This is also a solution to the second problem: lack of role models for new faculty.

A third problem is that fewer networking opportunities exist for women faculty and faculty of color. A possible solution is to emphasize collective socialization processes where women faculty and faculty of color participate in initiation rituals involving groups of new faculty. A fourth problem relates to the divergent demands placed on women faculty and faculty of color. A possible solution relates to key organizational gatekeepers, clearly spelling out what is expected of women faculty and faculty of color (sequential socialization processes). And finally, a fifth problem that the research literature has highlighted is that of additional demands placed on women faculty and faculty of color. A possible solution is to encourage diverse groups to become involved in different areas of campus life, but at the same time to make sure they are rewarded accordingly. This relates to divestiture socialization processes, where individual differences are affirmed. Table 3 is helpful in summarizing the discussion.

Faculty Women of Color

This section has discussed issues pertaining to women and faculty of color as if they are mutually exclusive categories. Obviously, faculty women of color exist in both social categories and face even more complex socialization dilemmas. Recently, different research efforts have documented the experiences of women of color. James and Farmer, for example, provided a series of essays about the struggles African-Americans face in academe (1993). Yolanda Moses offered

TABLE 3

Summary of Dimensional Analysis

PROBLEM	DIMENSION OF SOCIALIZATION	TACTICAL SUGGESTION
1. Inadequate anticipatory socialization	All six dimensions	Better mentoring during graduate training may be most imperative
2. Weak mentoring	Serial socialization	Provide better mentoring for new faculty
3. Fewer networking opportunities	Collective socialization	Implement group initiation processes
4. Divergent priorities	Sequential socialization	Spell out specific expectations
5. Additional demands	Divestiture socialization	Affirm individual differences and allow for flexibility

an overview of the experiences of black women in academe and provided an analysis of black women faculty (1989). McKay underscored some of the problems of being black and female:

One constantly feels the pressure of a double-edged sword: simultaneously, a perverse visibility and a convenient invisibility. The small number makes it easy for others to ignore our presence, or be aware of it. We are treated as blacks, on one hand, as women, on the other. We are left constantly taking stock of the landscape as different issues arise and we have to determine on which side, woman or non-white, we wish to be identified (1983, p. 145).

Further, a woman professor who is American Indian, for example, is highly visible, and even more demands are made. These demands often are made not for a concern for the individual, but because the person represents a specific group. Each is asked to serve on many committees. Each is asked to speak for various interests even when he or she may not desire to do so. Community groups also have needs that must be met. Women faculty of color, in many respects, face the greatest challenges and often find the least support.

Nieves-Squires discussed some of the dilemmas of "double discrimination": being both female and racially or ethnically different (1991). She noted that if Hispanic women are "too Hispanic," they may have difficulty succeeding in academe. "If her Hispanic peers consider her 'too Anglo,' she may lose their support. They may contemptuously refer to her as a 'coconut'—brown on the outside but white on the inside" (p. 6). The sense of double discrimination may go unrecognized by white women colleagues who sometimes exhibit an insensitivity toward cultural differences among women (Alperson 1975).

A Rationale for Socialization that Honors Difference
People of color represent diverse cultural groups, each with unique characteristics and ways of viewing and comprehending their social worlds. Melendez and Petrovich pointed out that "many attitudes and values of the university culture are at odds with the character of Hispanic interpersonal relationships, forms of communication, and sex-role expectations" (1989, p. 60). Additionally, cooperation and group cohesiveness are important values in Hispanic culture and in many ways antithetical to the competitiveness of academic culture (Nieves-Squires 1991). In discussing Latino faculty, Olivas noted that Latino teachers and scholars can make a difference through instruction, writing, service, and their characterization of social issues (1988). "They serve as useful irritants, interpreters of society, and role models for their students" (p. 8).

When an institution looks at difference as a strength rather than a weakness, a different view of the organizational world is developed. Such a view is imperative for the 21st century. It has become commonplace to speak of the need for the citizens of the United States to learn how to live in a multicultural society, because isolation will no longer be a suitable response in the future. A central role of postsecondary institutions is to help individuals function in such a world and to equip students with the skills to understand difference. Such a responsibility is not "only" for those of us who are different. As Lorde has pointed out, all too often individuals think that racism is a person of color's problem, or that lesbian and gay people only know how to deal with homophobia (1985). And yet, to build an institution where cultural difference is the norm, the organization's participants all must struggle to understand the concept of cultural difference. In doing so, socialization becomes not an experience where everyone must be homogenized, but a process that honors difference. Socialization is not an action where majority members try to equip minority members with the skills necessary to survive. Rather, socialization becomes a process amenable to cultural differences, which in turn enables all organizational members to become cultural learners.

If an organization tries to honor difference, then fundamental changes must take place. An institution, for example, cannot simultaneously expect people of color to contribute to scholarship in quantity and quality equal to that of their white male counterparts and at the same time expect people of color to fill manifold service needs that go unrewarded. The service roles filled by people of color are imperative to the eventual achievement of equal representation in academe. Therefore, institutions need to rethink how to reward such activities.

Ellsworth makes a case for a promotion and tenure process that honors difference when she highlights the cultural-identity issues involved in conducting research: "My experiences of the things I research are always shaped by the ways I negotiate my own identities and social positionings as a white, middle-class, gentile, able-bodied woman and lesbian in Madison, in the United States" (1992, p. 4). She went on to note that her research has always been grounded in the cultural expressions of women's communities. Relatedly, in recent years research has tended to demonstrate that men and women perceive their social worlds differently (Chodorow 1979; Gilligan 1982). For women, existing in a male-dominated educational sphere creates unique problems:

Socialization becomes not an experience where everyone must be homogenized, but a process that honors difference.

> In spite of the increase in the number of women students in higher education and professional schools, faculties, usually predominantly male, argue against a special focus on women students and resist open debate on whether women's educational needs are different from men's (Belenky et al. 1986, p. 5).

Clearly there is much resistance on the part of faculty to accept the notion that men and women might conceive of their social worlds differently. Such an assumption has significant implications for how faculty go about their teaching and research. Reynolds argued that women tend to adopt more cooperative views of social interdependence (1992). She went on to suggest that a cooperative view is brought by many women faculty to "the more competitive and individualistic views found in research-oriented faculty cultures" (p. 639). Reynolds also noted:

> *If a beginning professor enters the department with a view of social interdependence that is different from what he or she perceives to be the department's view, for example, a view that is more cooperative than competitive or individualistic, then it's likely that the professor will undergo acculturation rather than socialization* (p. 649).

Summary

Academic custom and precedence play a major role in the recruitment and retention of women and minority faculty and their overall socialization experiences (Exum et al 1984). Socialization that honors difference is about re-thinking custom and precedence. It is about an institutional willingness to change, to be flexible, to become more inclusive of cultural diversity. To recruit women and people of color without creating structures that encourage the re-shaping of the organizational culture is an assimilationist endeavor prone to failure, as evidenced by the poor attrition of faculty from diverse groups. As Simeone states:

> *It would not be sufficient for higher education simply to increase the numbers of women and minorities within the system if that system continues to be male-dominated in its policies, practices, epistemologies, values, methodologies, and structures* (1987, p. 21).

Increasing diversity demands structural changes, and socialization is a central ingredient of such change. What are some examples of socialization processes that honor difference? The concluding section develops a response to this question.

SOCIALIZATION FOR EMPOWERMENT: IMPLICATIONS FOR PRACTICE

The quality of higher education and the ability of colleges and universities, of whatever kind, to perform their respective missions is inextricably linked to the quality and commitment of the faculty (Schuster 1990a, p. 3).

Empowerment is a term whose currency perhaps has confused its meaning. In the 1980s everyone seemed to want to "empower" us—from Diner's Club to George Bush. Often, the speakers' use of "empowerment" meant little more than wanting us to use their services or vote for them. As we employ the concept here we return to the traditional sense of the term. Empowerment creates the conditions through which individuals and groups are able to gain control of their lives and prosper. No one can "empower" another person; for an individual or group to become powerful they must act on their own. Power is not something magical given to someone else. However, individuals do have the possibility of creating conditions that disable or support others.

Faculty socialization is an example of how individuals in an organization have the ability to create the conditions for empowerment. An institution where no mentoring or orientation program is in place or no thought has been given to the needs of tenure-track faculty is an organization where individuals must become empowered in spite of—rather than because of—the organization's culture. Conversely, a coordinated program that takes into account cultural difference, that develops activities to enhance professional training, and that exhibits concern for individuals is socialization for empowerment. At the same time, even the best of programs only create the conditions for empowerment, because individuals still must meet the challenges of tenure and professional advancement through their own initiatives.

In the remainder of this text we devote our attention to faculty development as a cultural strategy for shaping faculty socialization. Menges discussed faculty development as a process of becoming "fuller, larger, better. To develop is to elaborate, to articulate, to disclose" (1985, p. 181). Typically, faculty development has been conceptualized in terms of a psychological/developmental model; faculty growth is seen largely as a by-product of individual movement throughout the life cycle (Freedman 1979). Changes in faculty behavior are, in general, the result of individual changes, which typically are universal across individuals. In short, "The impetus to change lies within the individual" (Lawrence and Blackburn 1988, p. 23).

An alternative view of faculty development is described by Lawrence and Blackburn as a "socialization model" (1988). This view of faculty development reflects the perspective adopted here: Individual action and social contexts are mediated by an organization's culture. We have highlighted the cultural problems and challenges that different individuals and groups face when they work in a college or university. We have paid particular attention to the dilemmas encountered by tenure-track faculty, women faculty, and faculty of color. The remainder of the section divides in half: In the first part we consider responses to the problems faced with regard to anticipatory and organizational socialization; in the second part we delineate possible responses that pertain to the various dimensions of organizational socialization.

Faculty Development and Anticipatory Socialization

The kind of experiences one has prior to becoming a faculty member frame how an individual approaches his or her job. The culture of the discipline and the institution have several possible avenues for framing such experiences in a manner that will be helpful to the tenure-track faculty member. In particular, institutions that offer graduate training need to rethink the nature of graduate education. We are not calling for a dramatic upheaval of graduate training. We are suggesting that more conscious direction and structure be given to graduate education.

Increased calls for colleges and universities to be more concerned about teaching and learning suggests that graduate study needs to be altered if we are to adequately socialize the future profession. If institutions believe that service to the community is important, then that belief must be reflected in a graduate student's education. If we believe that faculty must be more adept at understanding issues of diversity, then some form of training and interaction ought to be created for students in graduate school. If the decline of community in academe is decried as harmful, then we must equip those who will enter academe with the skills necessary to build community.

What are the implications for such suggestions? At a minimum we are pointing out the obvious: We need to provide those who will populate the organization with the requisite criteria for work. Presently, graduate training is tied to the culture of the discipline. Individuals are trained about the nature of knowledge in a specific area. To recreate graduate education does not suggest that individual scholarship will decline or that programs must be changed entirely. Rather, institutional and disciplinary culture need to develop creative responses to the problems faced by academe.

For faculty to place higher emphasis on teaching, for example, they must be socialized in graduate school about the importance of teaching. The implications of such an idea may be that all graduate students who intend to become faculty need to take a course on teaching, or that a course might be co-taught with a faculty member. If service to the community is important, then an internship in one format or another could be developed. The clearest way to understand diversity is to ensure that one's program is diverse. Workshops on diversity specifically tailored to graduate students are another possibility. The way to develop scholars who exhibit concern about community is to develop community in graduate programs. Programs that are overly competitive, emphasize individual isolation over collaboration, or have no communal activities are socially created structures that are not necessary for the advancement of knowledge.

Anticipatory socialization also occurs through symbolic learning. A graduate student whose faculty mentor makes sexist jokes learns one lesson about diversity, and a member in a department where faculty regularly attend training sessions about cultural diversity learns another lesson. Faculty who involve themselves in the life of the community exhibit one symbol, and professors who do not speak with other colleagues offer another. A graduate program where faculty regularly talk about the importance of teaching suggests one idea, and a program where faculty exhibit an ongoing desire to avoid teaching offers another. The clearest examples of anticipatory socialization occur in graduate school, where students mimic the behaviors of their professors because they believe that is how faculty behave.

The culture of the discipline and its members also play a vital role in anticipatory socialization. It stands to reason that if graduate training is tied to the structure of the discipline, then the membership of the discipline must exhibit leadership in the reformulation of graduate training. Organizations that forcefully call for increased efforts for affirmative action strengthen institutional work in that area. A discipline that regularly holds workshops on teaching enables faculty to return to their campuses and continue the dialogue.

Disciplines and institutions also can strengthen anticipatory socialization with regard to research and scholarship. As noted, the world of publications and conferences is confusing and stressful to novices. When faculty co-author publications with graduate students, it helps soon-to-be-scholars understand the culture of research. A discipline that welcomes graduate students might include such support for professional development as travel money to conferences.

If one's ideas and presentational style at a conference are important, then one would expect that a graduate program ought to provide opportunities for graduate students to present papers in their programs before they "go public." If students need to understand how individuals evaluate articles for journals, then they should gain experience in judging articles of their peers.

There are a multitude of microscopic activities that may be developed with regard to anticipatory socialization. It surely is beyond the scope of this text to list all possible actions that an institution might take; however, we have provided an appendix that offers a few exemplary programs that might be found useful, as well as texts that speak about setting up such activities (see Appendix). Journal editors, for example, who suggest to a reviewer to add a non-binding graduate student reviewer to an article is developing anticipatory socialization. A faculty member who searches out ways to involve graduate students in cooperative tasks offers another form of anticipatory socialization. To the extent that academe wants to change in specific areas, it behooves its members to consider ways to socialize individuals to those new areas while they are in graduate school.

Faculty Development and Organizational Socialization
Entry
An institution concerned about socialization will consciously decide how it wants to structure the interview process for a candidate. The steps for an interview pertain to before, during, and after an interview. How might the institution write a job description so that an individual has a sense of the college or university's unique culture? Again, in general, job de-

scriptions—and the interview process itself—are remarkably tied to the disciplinary culture.

A candidate learns that college X needs an assistant professor to teach introductory courses in English composition and a graduate course in Victorian literature. Countless institutions will advertise such a need, but the advertisement will tell the candidate nothing about the unique nature of the specific college. A candidate could, for example, be asked to submit a brief statement about his or her philosophy of teaching. Such a request underscores that teaching will be important. An institution that writes that involvement in faculty governance is expected of all individuals highlights another distinctive aspect of the institution. An institution that values cultural diversity will not merely cite at the bottom of an announcement that a specific group is "strongly encouraged to apply," for virtually all institutions place such a comment. Instead, in the body of the text a specific comment will be made, and the types of journals and individuals contacted about the position logically will have connections with people of color.

If the organization's participants value consistency, then when a candidate sets foot on campus what was said in the application will be found. It is absurd for an institution to speak about the importance of teaching in an advertisement and then only to speak about research when a candidate arrives at the institution. A candidate might also get an initial idea about what it will take to get tenure, how it occurs, and who is involved.

We have mentioned the importance of the dean regularly speaking with tenure-track faculty. Obviously, the initial interview of a candidate by a dean is a good time to set the tone for future interactions. Again, if the dean does not intend to work with the candidate, then the individual should at least learn from the dean who will be involved. The department chair plays a similar role. Institutional services also are available about which the candidate should receive information. If there is a program to assist an individual's spouse or partner in finding employment, then that type of information can be sent in a packet of material to the individual. If there is a program in place which assists faculty of color, then a person of color should know that it exists and what kind of services it offers. Simply stated, as with the comments about anticipatory socialization, a multitude of activities provide a candidate initial socializing experiences, and to the extent possible an institution needs to consciously plan how to structure the interview for the candidate so that the individual receives the kinds of experiences the organization desires.

Role continuance

We commented in sections five and six about activities that might be developed for an individual who is on the tenure track or who has achieved tenure. We return now to the dimensions of organizational socialization to outline additional activities that might be developed.

Obviously, with each dimension both types of activities are possible. A tenure-track faculty member, for example, will have collective and individual experiences. Indeed, a person always will have unique individual experiences; what we emphasize, however, are those activities that an institution might consciously structure to improve the socialization of its faculty. These suggestions derive from the logic and literature of the preceding chapters and the schema built around faculty socialization. The suggestions, at times, overlap with one another to form a cohesive plan for the development of faculty socialization.

Collective—Individual (group or individual oriented)

- Develop ongoing orientation programs for tenure-track faculty to facilitate understanding of organizational culture.
- Utilize senior faculty in sharing the institutional history.
- Create informal networks where novices interact with senior faculty from other areas.
- Involve cohorts of new faculty as much as possible.
- Develop collaborative work environments and research opportunities.

Formal—Informal (isolated from or interwoven with organizational members)
- Develop a clear faculty development plan and make it known throughout the institution.
- Share as clearly as possible what one needs to do to achieve tenure.
- Create yearly review sessions for the novice with the department chair and the dean.

- Build informal activities for feedback and review.
- Encourage informal dialogue between novices and senior faculty.

Random—Sequential (unclear and ambiguous or clearly ordered)
- Clarify the kind of information needed in promotion and tenure dossiers.
- Provide accurate information to help tenure-track faculty adjust their priorities.
- Highlight the difference between yearly reviews and mid-point reviews.
- Provide dates for information submission.
- Develop specific methods for informing candidates of tenure-track decisions.

Fixed—Variable (specific or varying time frame)
- Recognize that socialization is an ongoing process, and develop programs for the different needs of faculty according to their age and professional development.
- Provide opportunities for reassessing individual interests and priorities.
- Provide feedback mechanisms at various times along the tenure-track route, mindful of individual differences.
- Make all time frames which affect the lives of faculty clear to them (eliminate surprise reviews or evaluations).
- Provide for individual flexibility in the tenure and promotion system based on unique circumstances (such as bearing or adopting a child).

Serial—Disjunctive (role models or no role models)
- Recognize that faculty socialization is an ongoing process which includes senior faculty.
- Develop faculty mentoring programs.
- Involve senior faculty in the socialization of novices.
- Develop rewards and incentives for senior faculty who serve as mentors.
- Do not overburden underrepresented faculty as mentors.

Investiture—Divestiture (affirming or transforming individual characteristics)
- Develop programs for senior faculty so they might become more aware of cultural differences.

- Have an office on campus specifically designed to meet the needs of faculty of color.
- Create informal networks for women and people of color.
- Involve faculty members in the implementation of faculty development programs.
- Include faculty input in planning faculty development programs.

Summary

Throughout this text we have sought a balance between delineating what the problems are with regard to socialization and how these problems might be overcome. Unlike certain dilemmas that confront higher education in the United States, the good news about the problem of socialization is that answers exist, and these answers do not have to fiscally bankrupt an institution to implement changes. Creating incentives for senior faculty to work with junior faculty is more a cultural issue than a fiscal one. An orientation program for new faculty involves dialogue and structure more than it does expensive equipment or outside consultants. A formal, yearly meeting with one's department chair and dean is a matter of time—not money. Of course costs are related, but if academe does not work more strategically in socializing faculty, the loss to the labor force is even greater; for an institution that desires to increase the number of women and people of color as faculty, the loss is even greater.

Ultimately, the challenge for an institution's participants is to be reflective about their organizational culture and how it goes about socializing its members. How do new members learn about the institution? What do they learn? How does the culture exclude some individuals and reward others? What might be improved? These are cultural questions that fundamentally revolve around issues of socialization. For institutions of the 21st century the struggle will not be merely to reflect on these questions, but to develop culturally specific strategies that enhance faculty socialization and, consequently, academic excellence.

APPENDIX

Innovative Faculty Development Ideas

- The University of Oklahoma has developed a semester-long faculty orientation program. The program involves weekly seminar-style meetings, and faculty participation has been high. During the 14-week program, a range of topics are covered: special teaching techniques, designing a course, evaluation of one's teaching, health and counseling services, time management, and the tenure-review process.

- The University of North Dakota has adopted a scholars' mentoring program where new faculty get a chance to work and network with some of the top faculty at the institution. One aspect of the program involves reading and then discussing the *Carnegie Report,* "Scholarship Reconsidered," where the goal is to get new faculty to develop their own understanding of what it means to be a scholar.

- The University of North Carolina at Chapel Hill has developed a guide to campus resources geared for the "perplexed UNC teacher." The guide offers suggestions on where one might find help about topics ranging from developing teaching skills to dealing with personal problems. UNC also has developed a guide to help faculty better supervise and train teaching assistants. Emphasized are issues related to defining the relationship between faculty and TAs, providing support and feedback for TAs, and teacher training resources.

- The University of Wisconsin system offers an annual "Faculty College" where faculty spend four days participating in teaching-related workshops. The most recent edition included programs on active learning, the ethics of teaching, fostering critical thinking, and collaborative learning.

- Augsburg College in Minneapolis has organized a gay/ lesbian study group for its faculty as well as a mentoring program connecting new faculty to faculty sponsors who provide guidance to their less-experienced colleagues.

- Western Carolina University has adopted a mentoring program designed to serve not only new faculty but senior faculty as well. New faculty benefit by learning more about their institution, while senior faculty benefit through the new roles and responsibilities they assume as mentors.

- Stanford has prepared an extensive handbook on teaching which includes a bibliography of works about college teaching. They also have organized an extensive videotape library where topics relate to course conceptualization and development, discussion leading, lecturing, and student-teacher interactions.

- In the spirit of Total Quality Management, the University of Colorado at Denver has implemented Student Management Teams designed to bring students and professors together to work on academic matters. The program emphasis is on how reflection and discovery can improve teaching and learning.

- The Great Lakes Colleges Association for the past 17 years has offered an annual Course Design and Teaching Workshop. The program targets not only beginning faculty who seek assistance but also senior faculty who hope to revitalize their teaching performance.

Key Resources for New Faculty

Boice, R. 1992. *The New Faculty Member.* San Francisco: Jossey-Bass.

Boyer, E.L. 1990. *Scholarship Reconsidered: Priorities of the Professorate.* Princeton, N.J.: The Carnegie Foundation for the Advancement of Teaching.

Fink, L.D. 1984. *The First Year of College Teaching.* New Directions for Teaching and Learning No. 17. San Francisco: Jossey-Bass.

Jarvis, D.K. 1991. *Junior Faculty Development: A Handbook.* New York: The Modern Language Association of America.

Schuster, J.H., and D.W. Wheeler. 1990. *Enhancing Faculty Careers: Strategies for Development and Renewal.* San Francisco: Jossey-Bass.

Sorcinelli, M.D., and A.E. Austin. 1992. *Developing New and Junior Faculty.* New Directions for Teaching and Learning No. 50. San Francisco: Jossey-Bass.

Weimer, M. 1990. *Improving College Teaching: Strategies for Developing Instructional Effectiveness.* San Francisco: Jossey-Bass.

REFERENCES

The Educational Resources Information Center (ERIC) Clearinghouse on Higher Education abstracts and indexes the current literature on higher education for inclusion in ERIC's data base and announcement in ERIC's monthly bibliographic journal, *Resources in Education* (RIE). Most of these publications are available through the ERIC Document Reproduction Service (EDRS). For publications cited in this bibliography that are available from EDRS, ordering number and price code are included. Readers who wish to order a publication should write to the ERIC Document Reproduction Service, 7420 Fullerton Rd., Suite 110, Springfield, VA 22153-2852. (Phone orders with VISA or MasterCard are taken at 800-443-ERIC or 703-440-1400.) When ordering, please specify the document (ED) number. Documents are available as noted in microfiche (MF) and paper copy (PC). If you have the price code ready when you call EDRS, an exact price can be quoted. The last page of the latest issue of *Resources in Education* also has the current cost, listed by code.

Aguirre, A. Jr. 1987. "An Interpretive Analysis of Chicano Faculty in Academe." *Social Science Journal* 24(1): 71-81.

Aisenberg, N., and M. Harrington. 1988. *Women of Academe: Outsiders in the Sacred Grove.* Amherst, Mass.: The University of Massachusetts Press.

Alperson, E.D. 1975. "The Minority Woman in Academe." *Professional Psychology* 6: 252-56.

American Association of University Women. 1989. *Women and Tenure: The Opportunity of a Century.* Washington, D.C.: Author.

Anderson, M.S., and K. Seashore Louis. 1991. "The Changing Locus of Control Over Faculty Research: From Self-Regulation to Dispersed Influence." In *Higher Education: Handbook of Theory and Research* (vol. VII), edited by J.C. Smart. New York: Agathon.

Anderson, W. Jr., H. Frierson, and T. Lewis. 1979. "Black Survival in White America." *Journal of Negro Education* 48: 92-102.

Anzaldua, G. 1987. *Borderlands.* San Francisco: Spinsters/Aunt Lute.

Association of American Colleges. 1985. *Integrity in the College Curriculum: A Report to the Academic Community.* Washington, D.C.: Association of American Colleges. ED 251 059. MF-01. PC not available EDRS.

Baldwin, R.G. 1979. "Adult and Career Development: What Are the Implications for Faculty?" In *Current Issues in Higher Education*, edited by R. Edgerton. Washington, D.C.: American Association for Higher Education.

Baldwin, R.G. 1990. "Faculty Career Stages and Implication for Professional Development." In *Enhancing Faculty Careers: Strategies for Development and Renewal*, edited by J.H. Schuster and D.W. Wheeler. San Francisco: Jossey-Bass.

Baldwin, R.G., and R.T. Blackburn. 1981. "The Academic Career as a Developmental Process." *Journal of Higher Education* 52(6): 598-614.

Banks, W.M. 1984. "Afro-American Scholars in the University." *American Behavioral Scientist* 27(3): 325-38.

Becher, T. 1987. "The Disciplinary Shaping of the Profession." In *The Academic Profession*, edited by B.R. Clark. Berkeley: University of California Press.

Becher, T. 1989. *Academic Tribes and Territories: Intellectual Enquiry and the Cultures of Disciplines.* Bristol, Pa.: Open University Press.

Becker, H.S. 1972. "What do They Really Learn at College?" In *College and Student: Selected Readings in the Social Psychology of Higher Education*, edited by K.A. Feldman. New York: Pergamon.

Becker, H.S., B. Geer, E.C. Hughes, and A.L. Strauss. 1961. *Boys in White.* New Brunswick, N.J.: Transaction Books.

Belenky, M.F., B.M. Clinchy, N.R. Goldberger, and J.M. Tarule. 1986. *Women's Ways of Knowing.* New York: Basic Books.

Bennett, W.J. 1984. *To Reclaim a Legacy: A Report on the Humanities in Higher Education.* Washington, D.C.: National Endowment for the Humanities. ED 316 074. 121 pp. MF–01; PC–05.

Bensimon, E.M., and A. Neumann. 1992. *Redesigning Collegiate Leadership: Teams and Teamwork in Higher Education.* Baltimore: Johns Hopkins University Press.

Bensimon, E.M., A. Neumann, and R. Birnbaum. 1989. *Making Sense of Administrative Leadership: The "L" Word in Higher Education.* ASHE-ERIC Higher Education Report No. 1. Washington, D.C.: Association for the Study of Higher Education.

Bergquist, W.H. 1992. *The Four Cultures of the Academy.* San Francisco: Jossey-Bass.

Bernard, J. 1964. *Academic Women.* University Park, Pa.: The Pennsylvania State University Press.

Bess, J.L. 1978. "Anticipatory Socialization of Graduate Students." *Research in Higher Education* 8: 289-317.

Birnbaum, R. 1988. *How Colleges Work: The Cybernetics of Academic Organization and Leadership.* San Francisco: Jossey-Bass.

Birnbaum, R. 1992. *How Academic Leadership Works: Understanding Success and Failure in the College Presidency.* San Francisco: Jossey-Bass.

Blackburn, R.T. 1985. "Faculty Career Development: Theory and Practice." In *Faculty Vitality and Institutional Productivity*, edited by S.M. Clark and D.R. Lewis. New York: Teachers College Press.

Blackwell, J.E. 1983. *Networking and Mentoring: A Study of Cross-Generational Experiences of Black Professionals.* Bayside, N.Y.: General Hall.

Blackwell, J.E. October 1984. *Increasing Access and Retention of Minority Students in Graduate and Professional Schools.* Paper presented at the Educational Testing Service's Invitational Conference on Educational Standards, Testing, and Access, New York, N.Y.

Blackwell, J.E. 1988. "Faculty Issues: Impact on Minorities." *The Review of Higher Education* 11(4): 417-34.

Blau, P.M. 1973. *The Organization of Academic Work.* New York: John Wiley & Sons.

Blumer, H. 1969. *Symbolic Interactionism.* Berkeley: University of California Press.

Boice, R. 1991a. "New Faculty as Colleagues." *Qualitative Studies in Education* 4(1): 29-44.

Boice, R. 1991b. "New Faculty as Teachers." *Journal of Higher Education* 62(2): 150-73.

Boice, R. 1992. *The New Faculty Member.* San Francisco: Jossey-Bass.

Boice, R. 1993. "New Faculty Involvement for Women and Minorities." *Research in Higher Education* 34(3): 291-341.

Bourdieu, P. 1977. *Outline of a Theory of Practice.* Translated by R. Nice. Cambridge: Cambridge University Press.

Bowen, H.R., and J.H. Schuster. 1986. *American Professors: A National Resource Imperiled.* New York: Oxford University Press.

Boyer, E.L. 1990. *Scholarship Reconsidered: Priorities of the Professoriate.* Princeton, N.J.: The Carnegie Foundation for the Advancement of Teaching. ED 326 149. 151 pp. MF–07. PC not available. EDRS.

Braskamp, L.A., D.L. Fowler, and J.C. Ory. 1984. "Faculty Development and Achievement: A Faculty's View." *Review of Higher Education* 7: 205-22.

Braxton, J.M. 1986. "The Normative Structure of Science: Social Control in the Academic Profession." In *Higher Education: Handbook of Theory and Research* (vol. II), edited by J.C. Smart. New York: Agathon.

Bronstein, P., E.D. Rothblum, and S. Solomon. 1993. "Ivy Halls and Glass Walls: Barriers to Academic Careers for Women and Ethnic Minorities." In *Building a Diverse Faculty*, edited by R. Boice and J. Gainen. New Directions for Teaching and Learning No. 53. San Francisco: Jossey-Bass.

Brown, M.H. 1985. "That Reminds Me of a Story: Speech Action in Organizational Socialization." *The Western Journal of Speech Communication* 49(1): 27-42.

Burke, K. 1966. *Language as Symbolic Action.* Berkeley: University of California Press. Sections reprinted in *Kenneth Burke, on Symbols and Society,* edited by J.R. Gusfield. Chicago: University of Chicago Press.

Caplow, T., and R.J. McGee. 1958. *The Academic Marketplace.* New York: Basic Books.

Carlyle, T. 1841. *Heroes and Hero-Worship.* London: Chapman & Hall.

Chaffee, E.E., and W.G. Tierney. 1988. *Collegiate Culture and Lead-*

ership Strategies. New York: American Council on Education and Macmillan.

"Characteristics of Full-Time College Professors, 1987." August 1992. *The Chronicle of Higher Education Almanac* 39(1): 28.

Chodorow, N. 1979. "Feminism and Difference: Gender Relation and Difference in Psychoanalytic Perspective." *Socialist Review* 46: 42-64.

Clark, B.R. 1963. "Faculty Culture." In *The Study of Campus Cultures,* edited by T.F. Lunsford. Boulder, Colo.: Western Interstate Commission for Higher Education.

Clark, B.R. 1970. *The Distinctive College.* Chicago: Aldine.

Clark, B.R. 1983. *The Higher Education System: Academic Organization in Cross-National Perspective.* Berkeley: University of California Press.

Clark, B.R. 1987a. *The Academic Life: Small Worlds, Different Worlds.* Princeton, N.J.: The Carnegie Foundation for the Advancement of Teaching. ED 299 902. 376 pp. MF–01; PC not available EDRS.

Clark, B.R., ed. 1987b. *The Academic Profession.* Berkeley: University of California Press.

Clark, B.R., and M. Trow. 1966. "The Organizational Context." In *College Peer Groups,* edited by T.M. Newcomb and E.K. Wilson. Chicago: Aldine Publishing.

Clark, S.M., and M. Corcoran. 1986. "Perspectives on the Professional Socialization of Women Faculty." *Journal of Higher Education* 57(1): 20-43.

Collins, M. 1990. "Enrollment, Recruitment, and Retention of Minority Faculty and Staff in Institutions of Higher Education." *Action in Teacher Education* 12(3): 57-62.

Commission for Educational Quality. 1985. *Access to Quality Undergraduate Education.* Atlanta, Ga.: Southern Region Education Board. ED 260 662. 19 pp. MF–01; PC–01.

Corcoran, M., and S.M. Clark. 1984. "Professional Socialization and Contemporary Career Attitudes of Three Faculty Generations." *Research in Higher Education* 20(2): 131-53.

Cross, W.T. 1991. "Pathway to the Professoriate: The American Indian Faculty Pipeline." *Journal of American Indian Education* 30(2): 13-24.

Deal, T.E., and A.A. Kennedy. 1982. *Corporate Cultures: The Rites and Rituals of Corporate Life.* Reading, Mass.: Addison-Wesley.

Dwyer, M.M., A.A. Flynn, and P.S. Inman. 1991. "Differential Progress of Women Faculty: Status 1980-1990." In *Higher Education: Handbook of Theory and Research* (vol. VII), edited by J.C. Smart. New York: Agathon

Dunn, D., M.A. Seff, and L. Rouse. Forthcoming. "New Faculty Socialization in the Academic Workplace." In *Higher Education: Handbook of Theory and Research* (vol. X), edited by J.C. Smart. New

York: Agathon.

Elay Group. 1988. "Entering the Lunchroom: Surviving in Academia." *Nursing Outlook* 36(2): 88-91.

Ellsworth, E. April 1992. *Claiming the Tenured Body.* Paper presented at the annual meeting of the American Educational Research Association, San Francisco, Calif.

Epps, E.G. 1989. "Academic Culture and the Minority Professor." *Academe* 75(5): 23-26.

Etter-Lewis, G. 1993. *My Soul is My Own: Oral Narratives of African American Women in the Professions.* New York: Routledge.

Etzioni, A. 1964. *Modern Organizations.* Englewood Cliffs, N.J.: Prentice-Hall.

Exum, W.H., R.J. Menges, B. Watkins, and P. Berglund. 1984. "Making It at the Top." *American Behavioral Scientist* 27(3): 301-24.

Feldman, K.A., ed. 1972. *College and Student: Selected Readings in the Social Psychology of Higher Education.* New York: Pergamon Press.

Feldman, K.A., and T.M. Newcomb, eds. 1970. *The Impact of College on Students.* San Francisco: Jossey-Bass.

Fink, L.D. 1984. *The First Year of College Teaching.* New Directions for Teaching and Learning No. 17. San Francisco: Jossey-Bass.

Finkelstein, M.J. 1984. *The American Academic Profession.* Columbus: Ohio State University Press.

Freedman, M. 1979. *Academic Culture and Faculty Development.* Berkeley, Calif.: Montaigne.

Frierson, H.T. Jr. 1990. "The Situation of Black Educational Researchers: Continuation of a Crisis." *Educational Researcher* 19(2): 12-17.

Garza, R.L. 1987-1988. "The 'Barrioization' of Hispanic Faculty." *Educational Record* 68(4)/69(1): 122-24.

Geertz, C. 1973. *The Interpretation of Cultures.* New York: Basic Books.

Geertz, C. 1983. *Local Knowledge.* New York: Basic Books.

Gilbert, C.T. 1990. *Minority Faculty Recruitment & Retention in Higher Education.* Paper presented at the U.S. Department of Education Special Hearing, Indian Nations at Risk Task Force, Arizona State Capitol.

Gilligan, C. 1982. *In a Different Voice.* Cambridge, Mass.: Harvard University Press.

Goffman, E. 1959. *The Presentation of the Self in Everyday Life.* Garden City, N.Y.: Doubleday Anchor Books.

Goffman, E. 1967. *Interaction Ritual.* New York: Pantheon.

Gouldner, A.W. 1957a. "Cosmopolitans and Locals: Toward an Analysis of Latent Social Roles-I." *Administrative Science Quarterly* 2(3): 281-306.

Gouldner, A.W. 1957b. "Cosmopolitans and Locals: Toward an Analysis of Latent Social Roles-II." *Administrative Science Quarterly* 2(4): 444-80.

Greenfield, T.B. 1973. "Organizations as Social Inventions: Rethinking Assumptions about Change." *Journal of Applied Behavioral Science* 9(5): 551-74.

Greenfield, T.B. 1980. "The Man Who Comes Back Through the Door in the Wall: Discovering Truth, Discovering Self, Discovering Organization." *Educational Administration Quarterly* 16(3): 26-59.

Hackett, E.J. 1990. "Science as a Vocation in the 1990s: The Changing Organizational Culture of Academic Science." *Journal of Higher Education* 61(3): 241-79.

Hamermesh, D.S. 1992. "Diversity within Adversity: The Annual Report on the Economic Status of the Profession 1991-92." *Academe* 78(2): 7-14.

Holland, D.C., and M.A. Eisenhart. 1990. *Educated in Romance: Women, Achievement, and College Culture.* Chicago: University of Chicago Press.

Horowitz, H.L. 1987. *Campus Life: Undergraduate Cultures from the End of the Eighteenth Century to the Present.* New York: Alfred A. Knopf.

Jackson, K.W. 1991. "Black Faculty in Academia." In *The Racial Crisis in American Higher Education,* edited by P.G. Altbach and K. Lomotey. Albany: State University of New York Press.

Jarvis, D.K. 1991. *Junior Faculty Development: A Handbook.* New York: The Modern Language Association of America.

Jensen, K. 1982. "Women's Work and Academic Culture: Adaptations and Confrontations." *Higher Education* 11: 67-83.

Joy, J., and R. Farmer. 1993. *Spirit, Space and Survival: African American Women in (White) Academe.* New York: Routledge.

Kimball, B.A. 1988. "The Historical and Cultural Dimensions of the Recent Reports on Undergraduate Education." *American Journal of Education* 96(3): 293-322.

Kuh, G.D., and E.J. Whitt. 1988. *The Invisible Tapestry: Culture in American Colleges and Universities.* ASHE-ERIC Higher Education Report No. 1. Washington, DC: Association for the Study of Higher Education. ED 299 934. 160 pp. MF–01; PC–07.

Kuhn, T.S. 1970. *The Structure of Scientific Revolutions* (2nd ed.). Chicago: University of Chicago.

Ladd, E.C. Jr., and S.M. Lipset. 1975. *The Divided Academy: Professors and Politics.* New York: McGraw-Hill.

Lawrence, J.H., and R.T. Blackburn. 1988. "Age as a Predictor of Faculty Productivity: Three Conceptual Approaches." *Journal of Higher Education* 59(1): 22-38.

Levi-Strauss, C. 1963. *Structural Anthropology.* New York: Basic Book.

Lorde, A. 1985. *I Am Your Sister: Black Women Organizing Across Sexualities.* Latham, N.Y.: Kitchen Table: Women of Color Press.

Lunsford, T.F., ed. 1963. *The Study of Campus Cultures.* Boulder, Colo.: Western Interstate Commission for Higher Education.

Luz Reyes, M. de la, and J.J. Halcon. 1991. "Practices of the Academy: Barriers to Access for Chicano Academics." In *The Racial Crisis in American Higher Education,* edited by P.G. Altbach and K. Lomotey. Albany: State University of New York.

Mager, G.M., and B. Myers. 1982. "If First Impressions Count: New Professors' Insights and Problems." *Peabody Journal of Education* 59(2): 100-06.

Mager, G.M., and B. Myers. 1983. *Developing a Career in the Academy: New Professors in Education.* Washington, D.C.: Society of Professors of Education. ED 236 127. 41 pp. MF–01; PC–02.

McElrath, K. 1992. "Gender, Career Disruption, and Academic Rewards." *Journal of Higher Education* 63(3): 269-81.

McHenry, D.E. 1977. *Academic Departments.* San Francisco: Jossey-Bass.

McKay, N. 1983. "Black Woman Professor—White University." Women's Studies International Forum 6(2): 143-47.

McLaren, P. 1986. *Schooling as Ritual Performance.* London: Routledge & Kegan Paul.

Mead, G.H. 1934. *Mind, Self, & Society.* Chicago: University of Chicago Press.

Melendez, S.E., and J. Petrovich. 1989. "Hispanic Women Students in Higher Education: Meeting the Challenge of Diversity." In *Educating the Majority: Women Challenge Tradition in Higher Education,* edited by C.S. Pearson, D. Shavlik, and J. Touchton. Washington, D.C.: American Council on Education and Macmillan Publishing.

Melillo, D. 1981. *Role Model and Mentor Influences on the Career Development of Academic Women.* Doctoral dissertation, United States International University.

Menges, R.J. 1985. "Career-Span Faculty Development." College Teaching 33(4): 181-84.

Merton, R.K. 1957. *Social Theory and Social Structure.* Glencoe, Ill.: The Free Press.

Merton, R.K. 1973. *The Sociology of Science.* Chicago: University of Chicago Press.

Moffatt, M. 1989. *Coming of Age in New Jersey: College and American Culture.* New Brunswick, N.J.: Rutgers University Press.

Moore, W. Jr., and L.H. Wagstaff. 1974. *Black Educators in White Colleges.* San Francisco: Jossey-Bass.

Morgan, G., P.J. Frost, and L.R. Pondy. 1983. "Organizational Symbolism." In *Organizational Symbolism,* edited by L.R. Pondy, P.J. Frost, G. Morgan, and T.C. Dandridge. Greenwich, Conn.: JAI Press.

Moses, Y. 1989. *Black Women in Academe: Issues and Strategies.* Project on the Status and Education of Women. Washington, D.C.: American Association of Colleges. ED 311 817. 29 pp. MF–01; PC–02.

Muller, C.B. April 1990. *Hidden Passages to Success: Academic Labor Market.* Paper presented at the annual meeting of the American Educational Researchers Association, Boston. ED 318 383. 26 pp. MF–01; PC–02.

National Governors' Association. 1986. *Time for Results.* Washington, D.C.: National Governors' Association.

Nieves-Squires, S. 1991. *Hispanic Women, Making Their Presence on Campus Less Tenuous.* Report for the Project on the Status of Women, Association of American Colleges, Washington, D.C. ED 334 907. 16 pp. MF–01; PC–01.

Olivas, M.A. 1988. "Latino Faculty at the Border." *Change* 20(3): 6-9.

Olsen, D. 1991. "Gender and Racial Differences among a Research University Faculty: Recommendations for Promoting Diversity." *To Improve the Academy* 10: 123-39.

Olsen D., and M.D. Sorcinelli. 1992. "The Pretenure Years: A Longitudinal Perspective." In *Developing New and Junior Faculty,* edited by M.D. Sorcinelli and A.E. Austin. New Directions for Teaching and Learning No. 50. San Francisco: Jossey-Bass.

Ouchi, W.G., and A.L. Wilkins. 1985. "Organizational Culture." *Annual Review of Sociology* 2: 457-83.

Parsons, T., and E.A. Shils. 1951. *Toward a General Theory of Action.* Cambridge: Harvard University Press.

Peters, T., and R. Waterman. 1982. *In Search of Excellence: Lessons from America's Best-Run Companies.* New York: Harper & Row.

Pettigrew, A.M. 1979. "On Studying Organizational Cultures." *Administrative Science Quarterly* 24: 570-81.

Pettigrew, A.M. 1983. "On Studying Organizational Culture." In *Qualitative Methodology,* edited by J. Van Maanen. Beverly Hills, Calif.: Sage.

Pfeffer, J. 1981. "Management as Symbolic Action: The Creation and Maintenance of Organizational Paradigms." *Research in Organizational Behavior* 3: 1-52.

Pondy, L.R. 1978. "Leadership is a Language Game." In *Leadership: Where Else Can We Go,* edited by M. McCall and M. Lombardo. Durham, N.C.: Duke University Press.

Rausch, D.K., B.P. Ortiz, R.A. Douthitt, and L.L. Reed. 1989. "The Academic Revolving Door: Why Do Women Get Caught?" *CUPA Journal* 40(1): 1-15.

Reynolds, A. 1992. "Charting the Changes in Junior Faculty: Relationships among Socialization, Acculturation, and Gender." *Journal of Higher Education* 63(6): 637-52.

Rhoads, R.A., and W.G. Tierney. 1992. *Cultural Leadership in Higher Education*. University Park, Pa.: Pennsylvania State University, National Center on Postsecondary Teaching, Learning, and Assessment. ED 357 708. 106 pp. MF–01; PC–05.

Riesman, D., and C. Jencks. 1962. "The Viability of the American College." In *The American College*, edited by N. Sanford. New York: John Wiley & Sons.

Rose, S.M. 1985. "Professional Networks of Junior Faculty in Psychology." *Psychology of Women Quarterly* 9: 533-47.

Rossides, D.W. 1984. "What is the Purpose of Education? *Change* 16(3): 14-21+.

Rothblum, E.D. 1988. "Leaving the Ivory Tower: Factors Contributing to Women's Voluntary Resignation from Academia." *Frontiers* 10(2): 14-17.

Schein, E.H. 1968. "Organizational Socialization." *Industrial Management Review* 9(2): 1-16.

Schein, E. 1985. *Organizational Culture and Leadership: A Dynamic View*. San Francisco: Jossey-Bass.

Schuster, J.H. 1990a. "The Need for Fresh Approaches to Faculty Renewal." In *Enhancing Faculty Careers: Strategies for Development and Renewal*, edited by J.H. Schuster and D.W. Wheeler. San Francisco: Jossey-Bass.

Schuster, J.H. 1990b. "Strengthening Career Preparation for Prospective Professors." In *Enhancing Faculty Careers: Strategies for Development and Renewal*, edited by J.H. Schuster and D.W. Wheeler. San Francisco: Jossey-Bass.

Schuster, J.H., and D.W. Wheeler, eds. 1990. *Enhancing Faculty Careers: Strategies for Development and Renewal*. San Francisco: Jossey-Bass.

Schutz, A. 1970. *Alfred Schutz on Phenomenological Social Relations*, edited by H.R. Wagner. Chicago: University of Chicago Press.

Schwartz, H., and S. Davis. 1981. "Matching Corporate Culture and Business Strategy." *Organizational Dynamics* 10(1): 30-48.

Simeone, A. 1987. *Academic Women: Working Towards Equality*. South Hadley, Mass.: Bergin & Garvey.

Smircich, L. 1983a. "Concepts of Culture and Organizational Analysis." *Administrative Science Quarterly* 28: 339-58.

Smircich, L. 1983b. "Organizations as Shared Meanings." In *Organizational Symbolism*, edited by L.R. Pondy, P. Frost, G. Morgan, and T. Dandridge. Greenwich, Conn.: JAI Press.

Smircich, L., and G. Morgan. 1982. "Leadership: The Management of Meaning." *Journal of Applied Behavioral Science* 18: 257-73.

Smircich, L., and C. Stubbart. 1985. "Strategic Management in an Enacted World." *Academy of Management Review* 10(4): 724-36.

Snow, C.P. 1959. *The Two Cultures of the Scientific Revolution*. Cambridge: Cambridge University Press.

Sorcinelli, M.D. 1988. "Satisfactions and Concerns of New University Teachers." *To Improve the Academy* 7: 121-33.

Sorcinelli, M.D. 1992. "New and Junior Faculty Stress: Research and Responses." In *Developing New and Junior Faculty*, edited by M.D. Sorcinelli and A.E. Austin. New Directions for Teaching and Learning No. 50. San Francisco: Jossey-Bass.

Sorcinelli, M.D., and A.E. Austin. 1992. *Developing New and Junior Faculty*. New Directions for Teaching and Learning No. 50. San Francisco: Jossey-Bass.

Spindler, G., and L. Spindler. 1989. "There Are No Dropouts Among the Arunta and Hutterites." In *What do Anthropologists Have to Say about Dropouts?*, edited by H.T. Trueba, G. Spindler, and L. Spindler. New York: The Falmer Press.

Study Group on the Conditions of Excellence in American Higher Education. 1984. *Involvement in Learning: Realizing the Potential of American Higher Education*. Washington, D.C.: National Institute of Education. ED 246 833. 127 pp. MF–01; PC–06.

Suinn, R.M., and J.C. Witt. 1982. "Survey on Ethnic Minority Faculty Recruitment and Retention." *American Psychologist* 37(11): 1,239-244.

Tack, M.W., and C.L. Patitu. 1992. *Faculty Job Satisfaction: Women and Minorities in Peril*. ASHE-ERIC Higher Education Report No. 4. Washington, D.C.: Association for the Study of Higher Education. ED 353 885. 147 pp. MF–01; PC–06.

Tierney, W.G. 1988a. "Organizational Culture in Higher Education." *Journal of Higher Education* 59(1): 2-21.

Tierney, W.G. 1988b. *The Web of Leadership*. Greenwich, Conn.: JAI Press.

Tierney, W.G. 1989. *Curricular Landscapes, Democratic Vistas: Transformative Leadership in Higher Education*. Greenwich, Conn.: Praeger.

Tierney, W.G. 1992a. "Building Academic Communities of Difference: Gays, Lesbians, and Bisexuals on Campus." *Change* 24(2): 40-46.

Tierney, W.G. 1992b. "Cultural Leadership and the Search for Community." *Liberal Education* 78(5): 16-21.

Tierney, W.G. 1992c. *Official Encouragement, Institutional Discouragement: Minorities in Academe—The Native American Experience*. Norwood, N.J.: Ablex.

Tierney, W.G., and R.A. Rhoads. 1993. "Enhancing Academic Communities for Lesbian, Gay, and Bisexual Faculty." In *Building a Diverse Faculty*, edited by J. Gainen and R. Boice. New Directions for Teaching and Learning No. 53. San Francisco: Jossey-Bass.

Tierney, W.G., and R.A. Rhoads. Forthcoming. "The Culture of Assessment." In *The Changing Labour Process in Higher Education*, edited by J. Smyth. London: Open University Press.

Tinto, V. 1987. *Leaving College: Rethinking the Causes and Cures of Student Attrition.* Chicago: The University of Chicago Press.

Toulmin, S. 1972. *Human Understanding* (vol. 1). Oxford: Clarendon Press.

Trice, H.M., and J.M. Beyer. 1984. "Studying Organizational Cultures through Rites and Ceremonials." *Academy of Management Review* 9(4): 653-69.

Tucker, A., and R.A. Bryan. 1988. *The Academic Dean.* New York: American Council on Education, Macmillan Publishing Company.

Turner, C.S.V., and J.R. Thompson. 1993. "Socializing Women Doctoral Students: Minority and Majority Experiences." *The Review of Higher Education* 16(3): 355-70.

Turner, J.L., and R. Boice. 1987. "Starting at the Beginning: The Concerns and Needs of New Faculty." *To Improve the Academy* 6: 41-55.

Turner, V. 1977. *The Ritual Process.* Ithaca, N.Y.: Cornell University Press.

van der Bogert, V. 1991. "Starting Out: Experiences of New Faculty at a Teaching University." *To Improve the Academy* 10: 63-81.

Van Gennep, A. 1960. *The Rites of Passage.* Translated by M. Vizedon and G. Caffe. Chicago: The University of Chicago Press.

Van Maanen, J. 1976. "Breaking In: Socialization to Work." In *Handbook of Work, Organization, and Society,* edited by R. Dubin. Chicago: Rand McNally College Publishing.

Van Maanen, J. 1983. "Doing New Things in Old Ways: The Chains of Socialization." In *College and University Organization: Insights from the Behavioral Sciences,* edited by J.L. Bess. New York: New York University Press.

Van Maanen, J., and S. Barley. 1984. "Occupational Communities: Culture and Control in Organizations." In *Research in Organizational Behavior* (vol. 6), edited by B. Straw and L. Cummings. Greenwich, Conn.: JAI Press.

Van Maanen, J., and E.H. Schein. 1979. "Toward a Theory of Organizational Socialization." In *Research in Organizational Behavior* (vol. 1), edited by B.M. Straw. Greenwich, Conn.: JAI Press.

Waggaman, J.S. 1983. *Faculty Recruitment, Retention, and Fair Employment: Obligations and Opportunities.* ASHE-ERIC Higher Education Research Report No. 2. Washington, D.C.: Association for the Study of Higher Education. ED 227 806. 73 pp. MF–01; PC–03.

Wallace, W.L. 1966. *Student Culture: Social Structure and Continuity in a Liberal Arts College.* Chicago: Aldine Publishing.

Wanous, J.P. 1992. *Organizational Entry: Recruitment, Selection, Orientation and Socialization of Newcomers* (2nd ed.). Reading, Mass.: Addison-Wesley.

Washington, V., and W. Harvey. 1989. *Affirmative Rhetoric, Negative*

Action: African-American and Hispanic Faculty at Predominantly White Institutions. ASHE-ERIC Higher Education Report No. 2. Washington, D.C.: Association for the Study of Higher Education. ED 316 075. 128 pp. MF–01; PC–06.

Weber, M. 1919 [1946]. "Science as a Vocation." In *Max Weber: Essays in Sociology,* edited by H.H. Gerth and C. Wright Mills. New York: Oxford University Press.

Weimer, M. 1990. *Improving College Teaching: Strategies for Developing Instructional Effectiveness.* San Francisco: Jossey-Bass.

Weis, L. 1985. *Between Two Worlds: Black Students in an Urban Community College.* Boston: Routledge & Kegan.

Whitt, E.J. 1991. "'Hit the Ground Running': Experiences of New Faculty in a School of Education." *The Review of Higher Education* 14(2): 177-97.

Widom, C.S., and B.W. Burke. 1978. "Performance, Attitudes and Professional Socialization of Women in Academia." *Sex Roles* 4: 549-62.

Wilkins, A.L. 1983. "Organizational Stories as Symbols Which Control the Organization." In *Organizational Symbolism,* edited by L.R. Pondy, P. Frost, G. Morgan, and T. Dandridge. Greenwich, Conn.: JAI Press.

Wilkins, A.L., and W.G. Ouchi. 1983. "Efficient Cultures: Exploring the Relationship between Culture and Organizational Performance." *Administrative Science Quarterly* 28: 468-81.

INDEX

A

academe

    cultures (or subcultures) in, 5, 6

    developmental culture, 6

    formal and informal bonds, 12

    freedom, importance placed on idea of, 12

    honesty, norms of, 12

    leadership, 6, 59

    negotiating culture focuses on distribution
        of resources, 6

    not done a good job socializing individuals
        to the organization, 15

    organization not adapted to diverse groups of people, 15

    profession, 11

acculturation process. *See* transformative socialization

actions, explicit and implicit, 6

affirmative action, 67

African-Americans faculty, 14, 22 *See also* Women

    feelings of isolation and alienation, 66

    lack of effective sponsorship of, 66

    struggles in academe, 68

    women, analysis of, 69

Aguirre (1987), 67

American Indian

    in professorate, 14

    woman professor, 69

anticipatory socialization, 23, 65

    inadequate, 68

    through symbolic learning, 75-76

Asian Americans in professorate, 14

Augsburg College in Minneapolis, 81

B

Becher (1987, 1988), 5

Bergquist (1992), 6

bidirectional

    philosophy of, 59

    socialization, 1-2

black faculty. *See* African-Americans faculty

Blackwell (1984), 65

blurred genres, 17

Boice (1991a, 1992), 36

Boice (forthcoming), 66

borders, cultural, 63

Brazil, 16

Brown (1985), 56

C

D

L

Ladd and Lipset (1975), 13
Latino faculty, suggested role of. *See* Hispanic faculty
Lawrence and Blackburn (1988), 74
leaders role in shaping culture, 4
leadership, demonstration of, 15
leave of absence, 59-60
lecture preparation, 37
lesbian people that only know how to deal with homphobia, 70
Lilly Endowment, funding from, xv
locals. *See* institution, commitment to
loneliness and isolation feelings, 36
Lorde (1985), 70

M

Madison, United States, 71
managerial culture, identified with organization, 6
McKay (1983), 69
medical students, training of, 24
Melendez and Petrovich (1989), 70
Melillo (1981), 66
Menges (1985), 73
mentoring, 58, 65. *See also* scholars' mentoring program
   and women
      as trail guides, 39, 54
      implies commitment and desire to learn from novice, 55
      need for experienced and caring, 28
      program for new and senior faculty, 81-82
      relationships, 66
Mexican-American community-related committees, 67
Mexico, 12
Moffatt (1989), 5
Moses, Yolanda (1989), 69
myths, definition of in faculty culture, 56

N

national influences, 9
Native American,
      demands on faculty as counselors and
         provide perspectives, 67
      Studies, 24
negotiating culture. *See* Academe
networking, 47
      for women and faculty of color, 68, 80
New Faculty, Key Resources for, 82-83
Nieves-Squires (1991), 69-70
non-conformist culture, 5

Rutgers University, 5

ASHE-ERIC HIGHER EDUCATION REPORTS

Since 1983, the Association for the Study of Higher Education (ASHE) and the Educational Resources Information Center (ERIC) Clearinghouse on Higher Education, a sponsored project of the School of Education and Human Development at The George Washington University, have cosponsored the *ASHE-ERIC Higher Education Report* series. The 1993 series is the twenty-second overall and the fifth to be published by the School of Education and Human Development at the George Washington University.

Each monograph is the definitive analysis of a tough higher education problem, based on thorough research of pertinent literature and institutional experiences. Topics are identified by a national survey. Noted practitioners and scholars are then commissioned to write the reports, with experts providing critical reviews of each manuscript before publication.

Eight monographs (10 before 1985) in the ASHE-ERIC Higher Education Report series are published each year and are available on individual and subscription bases. Subscription to eight issues is $98.00 annually; $78 to members of AAHE, AIR, or AERA; and $68 to ASHE members. All foreign subscribers must include an additional $10 per series year for postage.

To order, use the order form on the last page of this book. Regular prices are as follows:

Series	Price	Series	Price
1993	$18.00	1985 to 87	$10.00
1990 to 92	$17.00	1983 and 84	$7.50
1988 and 89	$15.00	before 1983	$6.50

Discounts on non-subscription orders:
• Bookstores, and current members of AERA, AIR, AAHE and ASHE, receive a 25% discount.
• Bulk: For non-bookstore, non-member orders of 10 or more books, deduct 10%.

Shipping costs are as follows:
• U.S. address: 5% of invoice subtotal for orders over $50.00; $2.50 for each order with an invoice subtotal of $50.00 or less.
• Foreign: $2.50 per book.

All orders under $45.00 must be prepaid. Make check payable to ASHE-ERIC. For Visa or MasterCard, include card number, expiration date and signature.

Address order to
  ASHE-ERIC Higher Education Reports
  The George Washington University
  1 Dupont Circle, Suite 630
  Washington, DC 20036
Or phone (202) 296-2597
  Write or call for a complete catalog.

1993 ASHE-ERIC Higher Education Reports

1. The Department Chair: New Roles, Responsibilities and Challenges
   Alan T. Seagren, John W. Creswell, and Daniel W. Wheeler

2. Sexual Harassment in Higher Education: From Conflict to Community
   Robert O. Riggs, Patricia H. Murrell, and JoAnn C. Cutting

3. Chicanos in Higher Education: Issues and Dilemmas for the 21st Century
   by Adalberto Aguirre, Jr., and Ruben O. Martinez

4. Academic Freedom in American Higher Education: Rights, Responsibilities, and Limitations
   by Robert K. Poch

5. Making Sense of the Dollars: The Costs and Uses of Faculty Compensation
   by Kathryn M. Moore and Marilyn J. Amey

1992 ASHE-ERIC Higher Education Reports

1. The Leadership Compass: Values and Ethics in Higher Education
   John R. Wilcox and Susan L. Ebbs

2. Preparing for a Global Community: Achieving an International Perspective in Higher Education
   Sarah M. Pickert

3. Quality: Transforming Postsecondary Education
   Ellen Earle Chaffee and Lawrence A. Sherr

4. Faculty Job Satisfaction: Women and Minorities in Peril
   Martha Wingard Tack and Carol Logan Patitu

5. Reconciling Rights and Responsibilities of Colleges and Students: Offensive Speech, Assembly, Drug Testing, and Safety
   Annette Gibbs

6. Creating Distinctiveness: Lessons from Uncommon Colleges and Universities
   Barbara K. Townsend, L. Jackson Newell, and Michael D. Wiese

7. Instituting Enduring Innovations: Achieving Continuity of Change in Higher Education
   Barbara K. Curry

8. Crossing Pedagogical Oceans: International Teaching Assistants in U.S. Undergraduate Education
   Rosslyn M. Smith, Patricia Byrd, Gayle L. Nelson, Ralph Pat Barrett, and Janet C. Constantinides

1991 ASHE-ERIC Higher Education Reports

1. Active Learning: Creating Excitement in the Classroom
   Charles C. Bonwell and James A. Eison

2. Realizing Gender Equality in Higher Education: The Need to Integrate Work/Family Issues
   Nancy Hensel

3. Academic Advising for Student Success: A System of Shared Responsibility
   Susan H. Frost

4. Cooperative Learning: Increasing College Faculty Instructional Productivity
   David W. Johnson, Roger T. Johnson, and Karl A. Smith

5. High School–College Partnerships: Conceptual Models, Programs, and Issues
   Arthur Richard Greenberg

6. Meeting the Mandate: Renewing the College and Departmental Curriculum
   William Toombs and William Tierney

7. Faculty Collaboration: Enhancing the Quality of Scholarship and Teaching
   Ann E. Austin and Roger G. Baldwin

8. Strategies and Consequences: Managing the Costs in Higher Education
   John S. Waggaman

1990 ASHE-ERIC Higher Education Reports

1. The Campus Green: Fund Raising in Higher Education
   Barbara E. Brittingham and Thomas R. Pezzullo

2. The Emeritus Professor: Old Rank - New Meaning
   James E. Mauch, Jack W. Birch, and Jack Matthews

3. "High Risk" Students in Higher Education: Future Trends
   Dionne J. Jones and Betty Collier Watson

4. Budgeting for Higher Education at the State Level: Enigma, Paradox, and Ritual
   Daniel T. Layzell and Jan W. Lyddon

5. Proprietary Schools: Programs, Policies, and Prospects
   John B. Lee and Jamie P. Merisotis

6. College Choice: Understanding Student Enrollment Behavior
   Michael B. Paulsen

7. Pursuing Diversity: Recruiting College Minority Students
   Barbara Astone and Elsa Nuñez-Wormack

8. Social Consciousness and Career Awareness: Emerging Link in Higher Education
   John S. Swift, Jr.

1989 ASHE-ERIC Higher Education Reports

1. Making Sense of Administrative Leadership: The 'L' Word in Higher Education
   Estela M. Bensimon, Anna Neumann, and Robert Birnbaum

2. Affirmative Rhetoric, Negative Action: African-American and Hispanic Faculty at Predominantly White Universities
   Valora Washington and William Harvey

3. Postsecondary Developmental Programs: A Traditional Agenda with New Imperatives
   Louise M. Tomlinson

4. The Old College Try: Balancing Athletics and Academics in Higher Education
   John R. Thelin and Lawrence L. Wiseman

5. The Challenge of Diversity: Involvement or Alienation in the Academy?
   Daryl G. Smith

6. Student Goals for College and Courses: A Missing Link in Assessing and Improving Academic Achievement
   Joan S. Stark, Kathleen M. Shaw, and Malcolm A. Lowther

7. The Student as Commuter: Developing a Comprehensive Institutional Response
   Barbara Jacoby

8. Renewing Civic Capacity: Preparing College Students for Service and Citizenship
   Suzanne W. Morse

1988 ASHE-ERIC Higher Education Reports

1. The Invisible Tapestry: Culture in American Colleges and Universities
   George D. Kuh and Elizabeth J. Whitt

2. Critical Thinking: Theory, Research, Practice, and Possibilities
   Joanne Gainen Kurfiss

3. Developing Academic Programs: The Climate for Innovation
   Daniel T. Seymour

4. Peer Teaching: To Teach is To Learn Twice
   Neal A. Whitman

5. Higher Education and State Governments: Renewed Partnership, Cooperation, or Competition?
   Edward R. Hines

6. Entrepreneurship and Higher Education: Lessons for Colleges, Universities, and Industry
   James S. Fairweather

7. Planning for Microcomputers in Higher Education: Strategies for the Next Generation
   Reynolds Ferrante, John Hayman, Mary Susan Carlson, and Harry Phillips

8. The Challenge for Research in Higher Education: Harmonizing Excellence and Utility
   Alan W. Lindsay and Ruth T. Neumann

1987 ASHE-ERIC Higher Education Reports

1. Incentive Early Retirement Programs for Faculty: Innovative Responses to a Changing Environment
   Jay L. Chronister and Thomas R. Kepple, Jr.

2. Working Effectively with Trustees: Building Cooperative Campus Leadership
   Barbara E. Taylor

3. Formal Recognition of Employer-Sponsored Instruction: Conflict and Collegiality in Postsecondary Education
   Nancy S. Nash and Elizabeth M. Hawthorne

4. Learning Styles: Implications for Improving Educational Practices
   Charles S. Claxton and Patricia H. Murrell

5. Higher Education Leadership: Enhancing Skills through Professional Development Programs
   Sharon A. McDade

6. Higher Education and the Public Trust: Improving Stature in Colleges and Universities
   Richard L. Alfred and Julie Weissman

7. College Student Outcomes Assessment: A Talent Development Perspective
   Maryann Jacobi, Alexander Astin, and Frank Ayala, Jr.

8. Opportunity from Strength: Strategic Planning Clarified with Case Examples
   Robert G. Cope

1986 ASHE-ERIC Higher Education Reports

1. Post-tenure Faculty Evaluation: Threat or Opportunity?
   Christine M. Licata

2. Blue Ribbon Commissions and Higher Education: Changing Academe from the Outside
   Janet R. Johnson and Laurence R. Marcus

3. Responsive Professional Education: Balancing Outcomes and Opportunities
   Joan S. Stark, Malcolm A. Lowther, and Bonnie M.K. Hagerty

4. Increasing Students' Learning: A Faculty Guide to Reducing Stress among Students
   Neal A. Whitman, David C. Spendlove, and Claire H. Clark

5. Student Financial Aid and Women: Equity Dilemma?
   Mary Moran

6. The Master's Degree: Tradition, Diversity, Innovation
   Judith S. Glazer

7. The College, the Constitution, and the Consumer Student: Implications for Policy and Practice
   Robert M. Hendrickson and Annette Gibbs

8. Selecting College and University Personnel: The Quest and the Question
   Richard A. Kaplowitz

1985 ASHE-ERIC Higher Education Reports

1. Flexibility in Academic Staffing: Effective Policies and Practices
   Kenneth P. Mortimer, Marque Bagshaw, and Andrew T. Masland

2. Associations in Action: The Washington, D.C. Higher Education Community
   Harland G. Bloland

3. And on the Seventh Day: Faculty Consulting and Supplemental Income
   Carol M. Boyer and Darrell R. Lewis

4. Faculty Research Performance: Lessons from the Sciences and Social Sciences
   John W. Creswell

5. Academic Program Review: Institutional Approaches, Expectations, and Controversies
   Clifton F. Conrad and Richard F. Wilson

6. Students in Urban Settings: Achieving the Baccalaureate Degree
   Richard C. Richardson, Jr. and Louis W. Bender

7. Serving More Than Students: A Critical Need for College Student Personnel Services
   Peter H. Garland

8. Faculty Participation in Decision Making: Necessity or Luxury?
   Carol E. Floyd

*Out-of-print. Available through EDRS. Call 1-800-443-ERIC.

Quantity **Amount**

_____ Please begin my subscription to the 1993 *ASHE-ERIC Higher Education Reports* at $98.00, 32% off the cover price, starting with Report 1, 1993. _____

_____ Please send a complete set of the 1992 *ASHE-ERIC Higher Education Reports* at $90.00, 33% off the cover price. _____

_____ Outside the U.S., add $10.00 per series for postage. _____

Individual reports are avilable at the following prices:

1993, $18.00	1985 to 1987, $10.00
1990 to 1992, $17.00	1983 and 1984, $7.50
1988 and 1989, $15.00	1980 to 1982, $6.50

SHIPPING: **U.S. Orders:** *For subtotal (before discount) of $50.00 or less, add $2.50. For subtotal over $50.00, add 5% of subtotal. Call for rush service options.* **Foreign Orders:** *$2.50 per book.* **U.S. Subscriptions:** *Included in price.* **Foreign Subscriptions:** *Add $10.00.*

PLEASE SEND ME THE FOLLOWING REPORTS:

Quantity	Report No.	Year	Title	Amount

Subtotal:	
Shipping:	
Total Due:	

Please check one of the following:
☐ Check enclosed, payable to GWU–ERIC.
☐ Purchase order attached ($45.00 minimum).
☐ Charge my credit card indicated below:
    ☐ Visa   ☐ MasterCard

Expiration Date _____

Name _____

Title _____

Institution _____

Address _____

City _____ State _____ Zip _____

Phone _____ Fax _____ Telex _____

Signature _____ Date _____

SEND ALL ORDERS TO:
ASHE-ERIC Higher Education Reports
The George Washington University
One Dupont Circle, Suite 630
Washington, DC 20036-1183
Phone: (202) 296-2597